Academic Library Website Benchmarks, 2013 Edition

ISBN: 978-1-57440-221-6
Library of Congress Control Number: 2013932097
© 2013 Primary Research Group, Inc.

TABLE OF CONTENTS

TABLE OF CONTENTS 3
LIST OF TABLES 4
THE QUESTIONNAIRE 18
SURVEY PARTICIPANTS 25
CHARACTERISTICS OF THE SAMPLE 27
SUMMARY OF MAIN FINDINGS 31
1. College Library Web Staff 48
2. Content Editing 70
3. Programming 94
4. Federsated Search 108
5. Website Marketing 118
6. Redesign 136
7. Library Website Budget 146
8. Web Statistics 155

LIST OF TABLES

Table 1.1: Does the college library have its own webmaster or web staff that is separate from the college website staff?...............48

Table 1.2: Does the college library have its own webmaster or web staff that is separate from the college website staff? Broken out by type of college...............48

Table 1.3: Does the college library have its own webmaster or web staff that is separate from the college website staff? Broken out by public or private status of the college...............48

Table 1.4: Does the college library have its own webmaster or web staff that is separate from the college website staff? Broken out by full-time equivalent student enrollment of the college...............48

Table 1.5: If the college does not have a separate webmaster or web staff, who runs the library website?...............49

Table 1.6: If the college does not have a separate webmaster or web staff, who runs the library website? Broken out by type of college...............49

Table 1.7: If the college does not have a separate webmaster or web staff, who runs the library website? Broken out by public or private status of the college...............49

Table 1.8: If the college does not have a separate webmaster or web staff, who runs the library website? Broken out by full-time equivalent student enrollment of the college...............49

Table 1.9: What percentage of the total man hours spent in running the college library website are provided by the following?...............50

Table 1.9A: College-wide web or Information Technology staff...............50

Table 1.9B: Library web or Information Technology staff...............50

Table 1.9C: Consultants, outsourced service providers, or other third parties...............50

Table 1.10: What percentage of the total man hours spent in running the college library website are provided by the following? Broken out by type of college...............51

Table 1.10A: College-wide web or Information Technology staff...............51

Table 1.10B: Library web or Information Technology staff...............51

Table 1.10C: Consultants, outsourced service providers, or other third parties...............51

Table 1.11: What percentage of the total man hours spent in running the college library website are provided by the following? Broken out by public or private status of the college...............52

Table 1.11A: College-wide web or Information Technology staff...............52

Table 1.11B: Library web or Information Technology staff...............52

Table 1.11C: Consultants, outsourced service providers, or other third parties...............52

Table 1.12: What percentage of the total man hours spent in running the college library website are provided by the following? Broken out by full-time equivalent student enrollment of the college...............53

Table 1.12A: College-wide web or Information Technology staff...............53

Table 1.12B: Library web staff or Information Technology staff...............53

Table 1.12C: Consultants, outsourced service providers, or other third parties...............53

Table 1.13: How many full-time equivalent library staff positions are devoted to the technological aspects of running the library website?........................54
Table 1.14: How many full-time equivalent library staff positions are devoted to the technological aspects of running the library website? Broken out by type of college........................54
Table 1.15: How many full-time equivalent library staff positions are devoted to the technological aspects of running the library website? Broken out by public or private status of the college........................54
Table 1.16: How many full-time equivalent library staff positions are devoted to the technological aspects of running the library website? Broken out by full-time equivalent student enrollment of the college........................54
Table 1.17: How is the library website handled on a day-to-day basis?........................55
Table 1.18: How is the library website handled on a day-to-day basis? Broken out by type of college........................55
Table 1.19: How is the library website handled on a day-to-day basis? Broken out by public or private status of the college........................55
Table 1.20: How is the library website handled on a day-to-day basis? Broken out by full-time equivalent student enrollment of the college........................55
Table 1.21: Which phrase best describes your library's web team?........................56
Table 1.22: Which phrase best describes your library's web team? Broken out by type of college........................56
Table 1.23: Which phrase best describes your library's web team? Broken out by public or private status of the college........................56
Table 1.24: Which phrase best describes your library's web team? Broken out by full-time equivalent student enrollment of the college........................57
Table 1.25: How many of each of the following does the library have for the internal communications needs of librarians or others who work for or with the library?........................58
Table 1.25A: Listservs........................58
Table 1.25B: Blogs........................58
Table 1.25C: eNewsletter........................58
Table 1.26: How many of each of the following does the library have for the internal communications needs of librarians or others who work for or with the library? Broken out by type of college........................59
Table 1.26A: Listservs........................59
Table 1.26B: Blogs........................59
Table 1.26C: eNewsletter........................59
Table 1.27: How many of each of the following does the library have for the internal communications needs of librarians or others who work for or with the library? Broken out by public or private status of the college........................60
Table 1.27A: Listservs........................60
Table 1.27B: Blogs........................60
Table 1.27C: eNewsletter........................60
Table 1.28: How many of each of the following does the library have for the internal communications needs of librarians or others who work for or

with the library? Broken out by full-time equivalent student enrollment of the college. 61
Table 1.28A: Listservs 61
Table 1.28B: Blogs 61
Table 1.28C: eNewsletter 61
Table 1.29: Approximately how many people outside your central library web staff typically enter page content in a given semester? 62
Table 1.30: Approximately how many people outside your central library web staff typically enter page content in a given semester? Broken out by type of college. 62
Table 1.31: Approximately how many people outside your central library web staff typically enter page content in a given semester? Broken out by public or private status of the college. 62
Table 1.32: Approximately how many people outside your central library web staff typically enter page content in a given semester? Broken out by full-time equivalent student enrollment of the college. 62
Table 1.33: If the library has one or more committees to oversee website policy in any respect (content, IT, graphics, etc.), how many total individuals sit on these committees? 63
Table 1.34: If the library has one or more committees to oversee website policy in any respect (content, IT, graphics, etc.), how many total individuals sit on these committees? Broken out by type of college. 63
Table 1.35: If the library has one or more committees to oversee website policy in any respect (content, IT, graphics, etc.), how many total individuals sit on these committees? Broken out by public or private status of the college. 63
Table 1.36: If the library has one or more committees to oversee website policy in any respect (content, IT, graphics, etc.), how many total individuals sit on these committees? Broken out by full-time equivalent student enrollment of the college. 63

Table 2.1: Which phrase best describes your use of content editing or management systems for the library website? 70
Table 2.2: Which phrase best describes your use of content editing or management systems for the library website? Broken out by type of college. 70
Table 2.3: Which phrase best describes your use of content editing or management systems for the library website? Broken out by public or private status of the college. 70
Table 2.4: Which phrase best describes your use of content editing or management systems for the library website? Broken out by full-time equivalent student enrollment of the college. 71
Table 2.5: Does your library website use a content management system? 72
Table 2.6: Does your library website use a content management system? Broken out by type of college. 72

Table 2.7: Does your library website use a content management system?
 Broken out by public or private status of the college..72
Table 2.8: Does your library website use a content management system?
 Broken out by full-time equivalent student enrollment of the college....................72
Table 2.9: If your library website does use a CMS, does it use the following?..............73
Table 2.9A: Drupal 73
Table 2.9B: e107 73
Table 2.9C: Joomla 73
Table 2.9D: Mambo 73
Table 2.9E: ModX 73
Table 2.9F: Plone 73
Table 2.9G: TextPattern 73
Table 2.9H: WordPress 73
Table 2.9I: Zoop 73
Table 2.10: If your library website does use a CMS, does it use the following?
 Broken out by type of college..74
Table 2.10A: Drupal 74
Table 2.10B: Joomla 74
Table 2.10C: Mambo 74
Table 2.10D: ModX 74
Table 2.10E: Plone 74
Table 2.10F: WordPress 75
Table 2.11: If your library website does use a CMS, does it use the following?
 Broken out by public or private status of the college...76
Table 2.11A: Drupal 76
Table 2.11B: Joomla 76
Table 2.11C: Mambo 76
Table 2.11D: ModX 76
Table 2.11E: Plone 76
Table 2.11F: WordPress 76
Table 2.12: If your library website does use a CMS, does it use the following?
 Broken out by full-time equivalent student enrollment of the college...................77
Table 2.12A: Drupal 77
Table 2.12B: Joomla 77
Table 2.12C: Mambo 77
Table 2.12D: ModX 77
Table 2.12E: Plone 77
Table 2.12F: WordPress 78
Table 2.13: How satisfied are you with your existing content management
 system? 79
Table 2.14: How satisfied are you with your existing content management
 system? Broken out by type of college. 80
Table 2.15: How satisfied are you with your existing content management
 system? Broken out by public or private status of the college. 80

Table 2.16: How satisfied are you with your existing content management system? Broken out by full-time equivalent student enrollment of the college..........81
Table 2.17: In the last full semester, approximately how many library personnel entered content into the college library website?..........82
Table 2.18: In the last full semester, approximately how many library personnel entered content into the college library website? Broken out by type of college..........82
Table 2.19: In the last full semester, approximately how many library personnel entered content into the college library website? Broken out by public or private status of the college..........82
Table 2.20: In the last full semester, approximately how many library personnel entered content into the college library website? Broken out by full-time equivalent student enrollment of the college..........82
Table 2.21: How satisfied are you with the consistency of style and brand presentation on your website?..........83
Table 2.22: How satisfied are you with the consistency of style and brand presentation on your website? Broken out by type of college..........83
Table 2.23: How satisfied are you with the consistency of style and brand presentation on your website? Broken out by public or private status of the college..........83
Table 2.24: How satisfied are you with the consistency of style and brand presentation on your website? Broken out by full-time equivalent student enrollment of the college..........84
Table 2.25: How easy is it to use and manipulate the following types of information or perform the following operations in your content management system?..........85
Table 2.25A: Position and manipulate videos..........85
Table 2.25B: Enter the same content to multiple locations on the site at the same time..........85
Table 2.25C: Easily enter charts, tables and other tabular data..........85
Table 2.25D: Check the functionality of page links..........85
Table 2.25E: Restrict a large number of content providers to be able to access only very specific areas on the site..........86
Table 2.25F: Provide a report of content changes in a specified period of time..........86
Table 2.26: How easy is it to use and manipulate the following types of information or perform the following operations in your content management system? Broken out by type of college..........87
Table 2.26A: Position and manipulate videos..........87
Table 2.26B: Enter the same content to multiple locations on the site at the same time..........87
Table 2.26C: Easily enter charts, tables and other tabular data..........87
Table 2.26D: Check the functionality of page links..........88
Table 2.26E: Restrict a large number of content providers to be able to access only very specific areas on the site..........88
Table 2.26F: Provide a report of content changes in a specified period of time..........88

Table 2.27: How easy is it to use and manipulate the following types of information or perform the following operations in your content management system? Broken out by public or private status of the college..89
Table 2.27A: Position and manipulate videos 89
Table 2.27B: Enter the same content to multiple locations on the site at the same time..89
Table 2.27C: Easily enter charts, tables and other tabular data...............................89
Table 2.27D: Check the functionality of page links..89
Table 2.27E: Restrict a large number of content providers to be able to access only very specific areas on the site 90
Table 2.28F: Provide a report of content changes in a specified period of time.........90
Table 2.29: How easy is it to use and manipulate the following types of information or perform the following operations in your content management system? Broken out by full-time equivalent student enrollment of the college..91
Table 2.29A: Position and manipulate videos 91
Table 2.29B: Enter the same content to multiple locations on the site at the same time..91
Table 2.29C: Easily enter charts, tables and other tabular data...............................92
Table 2.29D: Check the functionality of page links..92
Table 2.29E: Restrict a large number of content providers to be able to access only very specific areas on the site 92
Table 2.29F: Provide a report of content changes in a specified period of time.........93

Table 3.1: What is the most commonly used scripting language employed by the library website?...94
Table 3.2: What is the most commonly used scripting language employed by the library website? Broken out by type of college.....................................94
Table 3.3: What is the most commonly used scripting language employed by the library website? Broken out by public or private status of the college...........94
Table 3.4: What is the most commonly used scripting language employed by the library website? Broken out by full-time equivalent student enrollment of the college..95
Table 3.5: What percentage of the total script work done in Perl, PHP, CGI, JavaScript, and other scripting languages for the library website in the past year was done by the following sources? 96
Table 3.5A: Library information technology personnel 97
Table 3.5B: MLS librarians..97
Table 3.5C: College administration information technology department................97
Table 3.5D: Outside consultant or freelancer...97
Table 3.6: What percentage of the total script work done in Perl, PHP, CGI, JavaScript, and other scripting languages for the library website in the past year was done by the following sources? Broken out by type of college...98
Table 3.6A: Library information technology personnel 98

Table 3.6B: MLS librarians 98
Table 3.6C: College administration information technology department 98
Table 3.6D: Outside consultant or freelancer 98
Table 3.7: What percentage of the total script work done in Perl, PHP, CGI, JavaScript, and other scripting languages for the library website in the past year was done by the following sources? Broken out by public or private status of the college. 99
Table 3.7A: Library information technology personnel 99
Table 3.7B: MLS librarians 99
Table 3.7C: College administration information technology department 99
Table 3.7D: Outside consultant or freelancer 99
Table 3.8: What percentage of the total script work done in Perl, PHP, CGI, JavaScript, and other scripting languages for the library website in the past year was done by the following sources? Broken out by full-time equivalent student enrollment of the college. 100
Table 3.8A: Library information technology personnel 100
Table 3.8B: MLS librarians 100
Table 3.8C: College administration information technology department 100
Table 3.8D: Outside consultant or freelancer 100
Table 3.9: Does the library website use Cascading Style Sheets? 101
Table 3.10: Does the library website use Cascading Style Sheets? Broken out by type of college. 101
Table 3.11: Does the library website use Cascading Style Sheets? Broken out by public or private status of the college. 101
Table 3.12: Does the library website use Cascading Style Sheets? Broken out by full-time equivalent student enrollment of the college. 101
Table 3.13: Approximately what percentage of the library's cascading style sheets are in the "embedded styles" format? 102
Table 3.14: Approximately what percentage of the library's cascading style sheets are in the "embedded styles" format? Broken out by type of college. 102
Table 3.15: Approximately what percentage of the library's cascading style sheets are in the "embedded styles" format? Broken out by public or private status of the college. 102
Table 3.16: Approximately what percentage of the library's cascading style sheets are in the "embedded styles" format? Broken out by full-time equivalent student enrollment of the college. 102
Table 3.17: About what percentage of the routine content updates for the website are done through dynamic, database-driven web pages rather than through static pages? 103
Table 3.18: About what percentage of the routine content updates for the website are done through dynamic, database-driven web pages rather than through static pages? Broken out by type of college. 103
Table 3.19: About what percentage of the routine content updates for the website are done through dynamic, database-driven web pages rather

than through static pages? Broken out by public or private status of the college.. 103
Table 3.20: About what percentage of the routine content updates for the website are done through dynamic, database-driven web pages rather than through static pages? Broken out by full-time equivalent student enrollment of the college... 103
Table 3.21: Does the library website maintain an internal social bookmarking list or utilize an external bookmarking software or service (or else provide links to such a service)?.. 104
Table 3.22: Does the library website maintain an internal social bookmarking list or utilize an external bookmarking software or service (or else provide links to such a service)? Broken out by type of college........................ 104
Table 3.23: Does the library website maintain an internal social bookmarking list or utilize an external bookmarking software or service (or else provide links to such a service)? Broken out by public or private status of the college.. 104
Table 3.24: Does the library website maintain an internal social bookmarking list or utilize an external bookmarking software or service (or else provide links to such a service)? Broken out by full-time equivalent student enrollment of the college... 105
Table 3.25: Does the library website offer mashups devised by library staff?........... 106
Table 3.26: Does the library website offer mashups devised by library staff? Broken out by type of college.. 106
Table 3.27: Does the library website offer mashups devised by library staff? Broken out by public or private status of the college................................ 106
Table 3.28: Does the library website offer mashups devised by library staff? Broken out by full-time equivalent student enrollment of the college.................. 106
Table 3.29: Does the library website offer links to mashups devised by others?.. 107
Table 3.30: Does the library website offer links to mashups devised by others? Broken out by type of college... 107
Table 3.31: Does the library website offer links to mashups devised by others? Broken out by public or private status of the college............................ 107
Table 3.32: Does the library website offer links to mashups devised by others? Broken out by full-time equivalent student enrollment of the college.. 107

Table 4.1: How does your library handle federated search?.. 108
Table 4.2 How does your library handle federated search? Broken out by type of college.. 108
Table 4.3 How does your library handle federated search? Broken out by public or private status of the college... 108
Table 4.4 How does your library handle federated search? Broken out by full-time equivalent student enrollment of the college... 109

Table 5.1: Does the library have a presence on any of the following social networking or file-sharing sites? 118
Table 5.1A: Twitter 118
Table 5.1B: Pinterest 118
Table 5.1C: YouTube 118
Table 5.1D: Vimeo 118
Table 5.1E: Facebook 118
Table 5.2: Does the library have a presence on any of the following social networking or file-sharing sites? Broken out by type of college. 119
Table 5.2A: Twitter 119
Table 5.2B: Pinterest 119
Table 5.2C: YouTube 119
Table 5.2D: Vimeo 119
Table 5.2E: Facebook 119
Table 5.3: Does the library have a presence on any of the following social networking or file-sharing sites? Broken out by public or private status of the college. 120
Table 5.3A: Twitter 120
Table 5.3B: Pinterest 120
Table 5.3C: YouTube 120
Table 5.3D: Vimeo 120
Table 5.3E: Facebook 120
Table 5.4: Does the library have a presence on any of the following social networking or file-sharing sites? Broken out by full-time equivalent student enrollment of the college. 121
Table 5.4A: Twitter 121
Table 5.4B: Pinterest 121
Table 5.4C: YouTube 121
Table 5.4D: Vimeo 121
Table 5.4E: Facebook 121
Table 5.5: Does the library maintain any blogs for the benefit of those patrons who want to keep up with library news? 122
Table 5.6: Does the library maintain any blogs for the benefit of those patrons who want to keep up with library news? Broken out by type of college. 122
Table 5.7: Does the library maintain any blogs for the benefit of those patrons who want to keep up with library news? Broken out by public or private status of the college. 122
Table 5.8: Does the library maintain any blogs for the benefit of those patrons who want to keep up with library news? Broken out by full-time equivalent student enrollment of the college. 122
Table 5.9: Does the library maintain any listservs for the benefit of those patrons who want to keep up with library news? 123
Table 5.10: Does the library maintain any listservs for the benefit of those patrons who want to keep up with library news? Broken out by type of college. 123

Table 5.11: Does the library maintain any listservs for the benefit of those patrons who want to keep up with library news? Broken out by public or private status of the college. 123

Table 5.12: Does the library maintain any listservs for the benefit of those patrons who want to keep up with library news? Broken out by full-time equivalent student enrollment of the college. 123

Table 5.13: Does the library maintain any RSS feeds for the benefit of those patrons who want to keep up with library news? 124

Table 5.14: Does the library maintain any RSS feeds for the benefit of those patrons who want to keep up with library news? Broken out by type of college. 124

Table 5.15: Does the library maintain any RSS feeds for the benefit of those patrons who want to keep up with library news? Broken out by public or private status of the college. 124

Table 5.16: Does the library maintain any RSS feeds for the benefit of those patrons who want to keep up with library news? Broken out by full-time equivalent student enrollment of the college. 124

Table 5.17: Does the library produce any podcasts for the benefit of those patrons who want to keep up with library news? 125

Table 5.18: Does the library produce any podcasts for the benefit of those patrons who want to keep up with library news? Broken out by type of college. 125

Table 5.19: Does the library produce any podcasts for the benefit of those patrons who want to keep up with library news? Broken out by public or private status of the college. 125

Table 5.20: Does the library produce any podcasts for the benefit of those patrons who want to keep up with library news? Broken out by full-time equivalent student enrollment of the college. 125

Table 5.21: Does the library send out any email newsletters for the benefit of those patrons who want to keep up with library news? 126

Table 5.22: Does the library send out any email newsletters for the benefit of those patrons who want to keep up with library news? Broken out by type of college. 126

Table 5.23: Does the library send out any email newsletters for the benefit of those patrons who want to keep up with library news? Broken out by public or private status of the college. 126

Table 5.24: Does the library send out any email newsletters for the benefit of those patrons who want to keep up with library news? Broken out by full-time equivalent student enrollment of the college. 126

Table 5.25: How many separate RSS feeds or electronic newsletters about the library and its services can be subscribed to from the library website? 127

Table 5.26: How many separate RSS feeds or electronic newsletters about the library and its services can be subscribed to from the library website? Broken out by type of college. 127

Table 5.27: How many separate RSS feeds or electronic newsletters about the library and its services can be subscribed to from the library website? Broken out by public or private status of the college... 127

Table 5.28: How many separate RSS feeds or electronic newsletters about the library and its services can be subscribed to from the library website? Broken out by full-time equivalent student enrollment of the college................. 127

Table 5.29: What is the total number of subscribers to the electronic newsletters and RSS feeds offered by the library?.. 128

Table 5.30: What is the total number of subscribers to the electronic newsletters and RSS feeds offered by the library? Broken out by type of college... 128

Table 5.31: What is the total number of subscribers to the electronic newsletters and RSS feeds offered by the library? Broken out by public or private status of the college... 128

Table 5.32: What is the total number of subscribers to the electronic newsletters and RSS feeds offered by the library? Broken out by full-time equivalent student enrollment of the college. 128

Table 5.33: Does your website include personal customization features that enable end users to construct their own personal "my Library" identity, enabling them to save research strategies, favorite places, and/or other commonly used library resources?.. 129

Table 5.34: Does your website include personal customization features that enable end users to construct their own personal "my Library" identity, enabling them to save research strategies, favorite places, and/or other commonly used library resources? Broken out by type of college......... 129

Table 5.35: Does your website include personal customization features that enable end users to construct their own personal "my Library" identity, enabling them to save research strategies, favorite places, and/or other commonly used library resources? Broken out by public or private status of the college. 129

Table 5.36: Does your website include personal customization features that enable end users to construct their own personal "my Library" identity, enabling them to save research strategies, favorite places, and/or other commonly used library resources? Broken out by full-time equivalent student enrollment of the college. 130

Table 5.37: On average, approximately how many hours per month does the library spend working on search engine optimization for the library website?... 131

Table 5.38: On average, approximately how many hours per month does the library spend working on search engine optimization for the library website? Broken out by type of college.. 134

Table 5.39: On average, approximately how many hours per month does the library spend working on search engine optimization for the library website? Broken out by public or private status of the college............... 134

Table 5.40: On average, approximately how many hours per month does the library spend working on search engine optimization for the library

website? Broken out by full-time equivalent student enrollment of the college. 134
Table 5.41: Approximately how many hours per month does the library spend in updating its presence on Facebook, Twitter, YouTube, Pinterest, Vimeo, and other such social media sites? 135
Table 5.42: Approximately how many hours per month does the library spend in updating its presence on Facebook, Twitter, YouTube, Pinterest, Vimeo, and other such social media sites? Broken out by type of college. 135
Table 5.43: Approximately how many hours per month does the library spend in updating its presence on Facebook, Twitter, YouTube, Pinterest, Vimeo, and other such social media sites? Broken out by public or private status of the college. 135
Table 5.44: Approximately how many hours per month does the library spend in updating its presence on Facebook, Twitter, YouTube, Pinterest, Vimeo, and other such social media sites? Broken out by full-time equivalent student enrollment of the college. 135

Table 6.1: Within the past year, has the library launched any kind of major website redesign? 136
Table 6.2: Within the past year, has the library launched any kind of major website redesign? Broken out by type of college. 136
Table 6.3: Within the past year, has the library launched any kind of major website redesign? Broken out by public or private status of the college. 136
Table 6.4: Within the past year, has the library launched any kind of major website redesign? Broken out by full-time equivalent student enrollment of the college. 136
Table 6.5: Does the library plan any major redesign of the library website within the next two years? 137
Table 6.6: Does the library plan any major redesign of the library website within the next two years? Broken out by type of college. 137
Table 6.7: Does the library plan any major redesign of the library website within the next two years? Broken out by public or private status of the college. 137
Table 6.8: Does the library plan any major redesign of the library website within the next two years? Broken out by full-time equivalent student enrollment of the college. 137

Table 7.1: Is the budget for the library website a separate line item in the library's budget or is it considered part of the library's IT budget? 146
Table 7.2: Is the budget for the library website a separate line item in the library's budget or is it considered part of the library's IT budget? Broken out by type of college. 146
Table 7.3: Is the budget for the library website a separate line item in the library's budget or is it considered part of the library's IT budget? Broken out by public or private status of the college. 146

Table 7.4: Is the budget for the library website a separate line item in the library's budget or is it considered part of the library's IT budget? Broken out by full-time equivalent student enrollment of the college. 147

Table 7.5: About how much is in your library's annual central budget for the college library website? 148

Table 7.6: About how much is in your library's annual central budget for the college library website? Broken out by type of college. 148

Table 7.7: About how much is in your library's annual central budget for the college library website? Broken out by public or private status of the college. 148

Table 7.8: About how much is in your library's annual central budget for the college library website? Broken out by full-time equivalent student enrollment of the college. 148

Table 7.9: Total spending on the college library website in the past year has changed by approximately what percentage? 149

Table 7.10: Total spending on the college library website in the past year has changed by approximately what percentage? Broken out by type of college. 149

Table 7.11: Total spending on the college library website in the past year has changed by approximately what percentage? Broken out by public or private status of the college. 149

Table 7.12: Total spending on the college library website in the past year has changed by approximately what percentage? Broken out by full-time equivalent student enrollment of the college. 149

Table 7.13: Over the next year, you would expect that spending on the college library website will change by approximately what percentage? 150

Table 7.14: Over the next year, you would expect that spending on the college library website will change by approximately what percentage? Broken out by type of college. 150

Table 7.15: Over the next year, you would expect that spending on the college library website will change by approximately what percentage? Broken out by public or private status of the college. 150

Table 7.16: Over the next year, you would expect that spending on the college library website will change by approximately what percentage? Broken out by full-time equivalent student enrollment of the college. 150

Table 7.17: Over the past three years, how much did the library spend for outside programmers, consultants, and freelancers to alter, upgrade, or service in any way your academic library website(s) or your library social media sites? 151

Table 7.17A: Library website 151

Table 7.17B: Library social media sites 151

Table 7.18: Over the past three years, how much did the library spend for outside programmers, consultants, and freelancers to alter, upgrade, or service in any way your academic library website(s) or your library social media sites? Broken out by type of college. 152

Table 7.18A: Library website 152

Table 7.19: Over the past three years, how much did the library spend for outside programmers, consultants, and freelancers to alter, upgrade, or service in any way your academic library website(s) or your library social media sites? Broken out by public or private status of the college. 153

Table 7.19A: Library website 153

Table 7.20: Over the past three years, how much did the library spend for outside programmers, consultants, and freelancers to alter, upgrade, or service in any way your academic library website(s) or your library social media sites? Broken out by full-time equivalent student enrollment of the college. 154

Table 7.20A: Library website 154

Table 8.1: How many files are on your library's web site? 155

Table 8.2: How many files are on your library's web site? Broken out by type of college. 155

Table 8.3: How many files are on your library's web site? Broken out by public or private status of the college. 155

Table 8.4: How many files are on your library's web site? Broken out by full-time equivalent student enrollment of the college. 155

Table 8.5: How many unique visitors to the library website does your library site average weekly from September to May while college is in session? 156

Table 8.6: How many unique visitors to the library website does your library site average weekly from September to May while college is in session? Broken out by type of college. 156

Table 8.7: How many unique visitors to the library website does your library site average weekly from September to May while college is in session? Broken out by public or private status of the college. 156

Table 8.8: How many unique visitors to the library website does your library site average weekly from September to May while college is in session? Broken out by full-time equivalent student enrollment of the college. 157

Academic Library Website Benchmarks, 2013 Edition

THE QUESTIONNAIRE

COLLEGE LIBRARY WEB STAFF

1. Does the college library have its own webmaster or web staff that is separate from the college website staff?

2. If the college does not have a separate webmaster or web staff, who runs the library website?

    A. Library IT staff
    B. Library administration
    C. Central college website staff

3. What percentage of the total man hours spent in running the college library website are provided by the following?

    A. College-wide web or Information Technology staff
    B. Library web or Information Technology staff
    C. Consultants, outsourced service providers, or other third parties

4. How many full-time equivalent library staff positions are devoted to the technological aspects of running the library website?

5. How is the library website handled on a day-to-day basis?

    A. College IT staff does most technical work and the library handles content
    B. Library IT staff does most technical work and the library handles content

6. Which phrase best describes your library's web team?

    A. We do some content editing but don't have a full-time webmaster
    B. We have a webmaster and a little bit of help from others
    C. We have a webmaster plus a small staff of 2-5 FTE positions
    D. We have a webmaster plus a staff of more than 5 FTE positions
    E. More than one webmaster for more than one website

7. How many of each of the following does the library have for the internal communications needs of librarians or others who work for or with the library?

    A. Listservs
    B. Blogs
    C. eNewsletter

8. Approximately how many people outside your central library web staff typically enter page content in a given semester?

9. If the library has one or more committees to oversee website policy in any respect (content, IT, graphics, etc.), how many total individuals sit on these committees?

10. Describe the relationship between those at the library who run the website and those who may run library-related media sites on Facebook, YouTube, Pinterest, and other social media sites. Are they more or less run by the same parties? Are the staffs different? Are the submission and posting rules the same or different? How so?

CONTENT EDITING

11. Which phrase best describes your use of content editing or management systems for the library website?

    A. Purchased a commercial system for the library
    B. System provided by the college web staff
    C. Adapted an open-source alternative
    D. Program our own system

12. Does your library website use a content management system?

13. If your library website does use a CMS, does it use the following?

    A. Drupal
    B. e107
    C. Joomla
    D. Mambo
    E. ModX
    F. Plone
    G. TextPattern
    H. WordPress
    I. Zoop

14. If the library uses a CMS not listed above, please specify.

15. How satisfied are you with your existing content management system?

    A. Quite satisfied
    B. Satisfied
    C. Not completely satisfied

D. We plan to change systems

16. In the last full semester, approximately how many library personnel entered content into the college library website?

17. How satisfied are you with the consistence of style and brand presentation on your website?

    A. Not an important goal
    B. Not very satisfied
    C. Somewhat satisfied
    D. Generally satisfied

18. How easy is it to use and manipulate the following types of information or perform the following operations in your content management system?

    A. Position and manipulate videos
    B. Enter the same content to multiple locations on the site at the same time
    C. Easily enter charts, tables and other tabular data
    D. Check the functionality of page links
    E. Restrict a large number of content providers to be able to access only very specific areas of the site
    F. Provide a report of content changes in a specified period of time

PROGRAMMING

19. What is the most commonly used scripting language employed by the library website?

    A. Perl
    B. JavaScript
    C. CGI
    D. PHP
    E. Other

20. If the library website uses a scripting language not listed above, please specify.

21. What percentage of the total script work done in Perl, PHP, CGI, JavaScript, and other scripting languages for the library website in the past year was done by the following sources?

    A. Library information technology personnel
    B. MLS librarians

C. College administration information technology department
D. Outside consultant or freelancer

22. Does the library website use Cascading Style Sheets?

    A. Not at all
    B. Moderately
    C. Extensively
    D. Not sure

23. Approximately what percentage of the library's cascading style sheets are in the "embedded styles" format?

24. About what percentage of the routine content updates for the website are done through dynamic, database-driven web pages rather than through static pages?

25. Does the library website maintain an internal social bookmarking list or utilize an external bookmarking software or service (or else provide links to such a service)?

    A. Internal social bookmarking lists
    B. External bookmarking software or service
    C. Links to bookmarking software or service

26. Does the library website offer mashups devised by library staff?

27. Does the library website offer links to mashups devised by others?

FEDERATED SEARCH

28. How does your library handle federated search?

    A. Uses a commercial discovery platform
    B. Devised our own federated search engine
    C. Does not emphasize federated search

29. Has your library altered the size, shape, graphic design, or placement of your website search boxes in recent years? If so, why? What have been the results?

30. Describe what your library has done in the past three years to change its search interface to make it more attractive and effective for end users.

WEBSITE MARKETING

31. Does the library have a presence on any of the following social networking or file-sharing sites?

    A. Twitter
    B. Pinterest
    C. YouTube
    D. Vimeo
    E. Facebook

32. Does the library maintain any of the following for the benefit of those patrons who want to keep up with library news?

    A. Blogs
    B. Listservs
    C. RSS feeds
    D. Podcasts
    E. Email newsletters

33. How many separate RSS feeds or electronic newsletters about the library and its services can be subscribed to from the library website?

34. What is the total number of subscribers to the electronic newsletters and RSS feeds offered by the library?

35. Does your website include personal customization features that enable end users to construct their own personal "my Library" identity, enabling them to save research strategies, favourite places, and/or other commonly used library resources.

    A. Yes
    B. No
    C. No, but we are planning on it

36. Describe what steps the library has taken, if any, to customize or personalize the library website.

37. On average, approximately how many hours per month does the library spend working on search engine optimization for the library website?

38. Approximately how many hours per month does the library spend in updating its presence on Facebook, Twitter, YouTube, Pinterest, Vimeo, and other such social media sites?

REDESIGN

39. Within the past year, has the library launched any kind of major website redesign?

40. Does the library plan any major redesign of the library website within the next two years?

41. If the library is planning a redesign within the next two years, what do you think that the major goals of this redesign might be?

42. If the library has done a redesign within the past two years, what did this redesign accomplish?

43. What is the single best product or idea that you have discovered in recent years that has most helped you to improve the library website?

LIBRARY WEBSITE BUDGET

44. Is the budget for the library website a separate line item in the library's budget or is it considered part of the library's IT budget?

    A. Separate line item in the library budget
    B. Part of the library IT budget
    C. Part of the college IT budget

45. About how much is in your library's annual central budget for the college library website?

46. Total spending on the college library website in the past year has changed by approximately what percentage?

47. Over the next year, you would expect that spending on the college library website will change by approximately what percentage?[*]

48. Over the past three years, how much did the library spend for outside programmers, consultants, and freelancers to alter, upgrade, or service in any way your academic library website(s) or your library social media sites?

---

[*] Includes spending on salaries, technology, consultants, content development, etc.

WEB STATISTICS

49. How many files are on your library's web site?

50. How many unique visitors to the library website does your library site average weekly from September to May while college is in session?

SURVEY PARTICIPANTS

Augustana College (South Dakota)
Baton Rouge Community College
Cal Poly Pomona
Central Wyoming College
Charter College
Chesapeake College
Coastal Carolina University
College of the Holy Cross
College of the Rockies
Colorado State University – Pueblo
Community College of Vermont/Vermont Technical College
Creighton University
Dine College
Florida Keys Community College
Franklin & Marshall College
Gogebic Community College
Golden Gate Baptist Theological Seminary
Illinois Institute of Technology
Kendall College
Laguna College of Art + Design
Lansing Community College
Las Positas College
Lehman College – CUNY
Long Beach City College
Los Medanos College
Michigan State University
Mott Community College
Neosho County Community College
New College of Florida
New York City College of Technology – CUNY
North Dakota State College of Science
Ohio University
Ozarks Technical Community College
Pitt Community College
Portland Community College
Princeton University
Sam Houston State University
Santa Rosa Junior College
Sheridan College
Southwest Baptist University
SUNY Potsdam

Tarleton State University
Texas A&M University – Kingsville
Texas A&M University – Commerce
Trocaire College
The University of Akron
University of Alaska Anchorage
University of Colorado at Colorado Springs
University of Dayton
University of Detroit Mercy
University of Illinois at Chicago
University of Michigan
University of New Hampshire
University of Northern Iowa
University of Oregon
University of South Alabama
Wheelock College

CHARACTERISTICS OF THE SAMPLE

Overall sample size: 57

By Type of College
Community college	22
4-year/MA-granting college	19
PhD-granting college/Research university	16

By Public or Private Status
Public	42
Private	15

By Full-Time Equivalent Student Enrollment
Less than 2,500	16
2,500 to 7,499	15
7.500 to 14,999	13
15,000 or more	13

Public or private status of the college, broken out by type of college.

Type of College	Public	Private
Community college	86.36%	13.64%
4-year/MA-granting college	52.63%	47.37%
PhD-granting college/Research university	81.25%	18.75%

Public or private status of the college, broken out by full-time equivalent student enrollment of the college.

Enrollment	Public	Private
Less than 2,500	56.25%	43.75%
2,500 to 7,499	60.00%	40.00%
7,500 to 14,999	92.31%	7.69%
15,000 or more	92.31%	7.69%

Type of college, broken out by public or private status of the college.

Public or Private	Community college	4-year/MA-granting college	PhD-granting college/Research university
Public	45.24%	23.81%	30.95%
Private	20.00%	60.00%	20.00%

Type of college, broken out by full-time equivalent student enrollment of the college.

Enrollment	Community college	4-year/MA-granting college	PhD-granting college/Research university
Less than 2,500	56.25%	37.50%	6.25%
2,500 to 7,499	33.33%	46.67%	20.00%
7,500 to 14,999	38.46%	30.77%	30.77%
15,000 or more	23.08%	15.38%	61.54%

Full-time equivalent student enrollment of the college, broken out by public or private status of the college.

Public or Private	Less than 2,500	2,500 to 7,499	7,500 to 14,999	15,000 or more
Public	21.43%	21.43%	28.57%	28.57%
Private	46.67%	40.00%	6.67%	6.67%

Full-time equivalent student enrollment of the college, broken out by type of college.

Type of College	Less than 2,500	2,500 to 7,499	7,500 to 14,999	15,000 or more
Community college	40.91%	22.73%	22.73%	13.64%
4-year/MA-granting college	31.58%	36.84%	21.05%	10.53%
PhD-granting college/Research university	6.25%	18.75%	25.00%	50.00%

SUMMARY OF MAIN FINDINGS

COLLEGE LIBRARY WEB STAFF

Webmasters

61.4 percent of libraries in the sample have their own webmasters (or web staffs) that are separate from the college website staff. These separate webmasters are much more common at 4-year/MA-granting colleges (73.68 percent) and PhD-granting colleges/research universities (81.25 percent), as just 36.36 percent of community colleges have these webmasters. The split between public and private schools, however, is nearly identical, with the former having 61.9 percent and the latter an even 60 percent. As total student enrollment increases, so too does the likelihood of the library having its own webmaster: whereas only 37.5 percent of those libraries at schools with less than 2,500 students have a separate webmaster, this figure jumps to 60 percent for the next enrollment range (2,500 to 7,499 students) before topping out at 84.62 percent for those schools with 15,000 or more students.

Running the Library Website

Among those libraries that do not have a separate webmaster or web staff, a hair more than half (52.38 percent) of them say the library website is run by library IT staff. 28.57 percent say the website is run by library administration, while the remaining 19.05 percent say it is run by a central college website staff. Two-thirds of these PhD-granting colleges and research universities say the website is run by library IT staff and none of them say it is run by the central college website staff. Again the split between public and private schools is fairly even, with 53.33 percent of the former saying it's run by library IT staff and exactly half of the latter saying the same. 75 percent of those libraries at schools in the "7,500 to 14,999" enrollment range have the library website run by library IT, compared to just 33.33 percent of those in the "less than 2,500" range.

Survey participants estimate that a mean of 83 percent of the total man hours spent running the library website are spent by library web or IT staff. The median is even higher at 99 percent, and 33 participants responded at 95 percent or higher. College-wide web or IT staff account for a mean of 14.7 percent of the work done here, while an average of just 2.25 percent of total man hours is attributed to consultants, outsourced service providers, and other third parties. The bulk of these participants that allocate any time at all to these third parties are private schools and 4-year/MA-granting colleges with less than 2,500 students. In fact, as student enrollment increases, the libraries in the sample dedicate higher percentages of this work to the library web or IT staff, from a mean of 68.47 percent for those in the "less than 2,500" range up to a mean of 94.46 percent for those in the "15,000 or more" range.

According to the survey participants, a mean of 1.42 full-time equivalent library staff positions are devoted to the technological aspects of running the library website. The median is 1, and the range is from 0 to 20. PhD-granting colleges and research universities devote the most FTE positions, a mean of 2.66, while the community colleges in the sample have a mean of just 0.71. However, this is inflated by one participant's answer of 20 when in fact no other participant devotes more than 4 FTE staff positions to running the library website. This participant with 20 FTE staff positions is a public school with 15,000 or more students.

Day-to-Day Operation

For two-thirds of the libraries in the sample, the technical work of the library website is handled on a day-to-day basis mostly by library IT staff, while the remaining one third says the college IT staff handles these duties. Broken out by type of college, these two departments are split evenly for the community colleges. On the other hand, 87.5 percent of PhD-granting colleges and research universities say the library IT staff handles the day-to-day operations. Whereas 43.75 percent of those libraries at schools with less than 2,500 students say the college IT staff is in charge of this, compare this to just 15.38 percent of those libraries in the "15,000 or more" enrollment range.

Library Web Team

When asked to describe their library's web team, just a bit more than half (52.73 percent) of survey participants say they have a webmaster and also get a little bit of help from others. 29.09 percent say they handle some content editing on their own although they do not have a full-time webmaster. No libraries in the sample have a webmaster plus a staff of more than five FTE positions, and just 1.82 percent say they have more than one webmaster for more than one website. Half of all community colleges in the sample do not have a full-time webmaster, compared to just 16.67 of 4-year/MA-granting colleges and 13.33 percent of PhD-granting colleges and research universities.

Listservs

The libraries in the sample have a mean of 4.67 listservs for the internal communications needs of its librarians and all others who work for or with the library. However, this mean is inflated somewhat by one participant's response of 100, as only seven participants have more than three such listservs. The overall median is 0. This one participant with 100 listservs is a public PhD-granting college or research university with 15,000 students or more. 32 participants do not have any such listservs.

Blogs

Even fewer libraries maintain blogs to serve these purposes, as just one participant has more than two of these (of which they have 25). The overall sample mean is 1, the median is 0, and 26 participants say they do not have any such blogs. No private school library in the sample has more than 1, for a mean of 0.44, while the mean for public schools is 1.15. Still, the medians in both instances is 0. Broken out by total student enrollment, the only category where the median is not 0 is the top enrollment range (15,000 or more students), where the median is 1 (and the median is 2.67).

eNewsletters

Rarer still is the eNewsletter, as just 8 participants have any eNewsletters for the purposes of internal communications among library staff, and all of which have just 1. None of these are community colleges, nor are any of them schools with less than 2,500 students.

Content Entry

According to our survey participants, a mean of 6.79 people outside the central library website enter page content in a given semester. The median, however, is zero, as this mean is inflated by two participants' responses of 100 and 75, respectively. No other participant answered more than 32.5 and 39 participants answered less than five. The PhD-granting colleges and research universities posted the highest mean at 18 as well as the highest median at 4. All other medians in this category were zero. Broken out by public and private status, the public schools have a mean of 7.97 people outside the library web staff enter page content in a semester, while private schools have a mean of just 3.23 such people. The biggest anomaly occurs when the data is broken out by full-time student enrollment: well all categories under 15,000 students posted means below 4, the mean for the "15,000 or more" enrollment range was 20.88.

Website Policy Committees

For those survey participants with one or more committees to oversee website policy in any respect (i.e. content, IT, graphics), the mean number of individuals sitting on these committees is 7.08. The median is six, and the range is from one to 20. Community colleges posted the lowest mean among all types of colleges with a mean of 5.86. 4-year/MA-granting colleges had a mean of 7, while PhD-granting colleges and research universities had a mean of 7.91 individuals on these committees. Broken out by public and private status, public schools had more individuals on these committees, a mean of 7.36, compared to a mean of 5.5 for private schools. The means for all enrollment ranges up to 14,999 students are between 6 and 6.33, but this mean jumps to 8.17 for those libraries at schools with 15,000 or more students.

CONTENT EDITING

CMS for the Library Website

31.58 percent of survey participants say their content management system was provided by the college web staff, while 24.56 percent say they adapted an open-source alternative. 22.81 percent programmed their own system, while just 10.53 percent purchased a commercial system for the library. Broken out by type of college, the community colleges were the mostly likely to use a system provided by the college web staff, as 40.91 percent of them did, while 36.84 percent of 4-year and MA-granting colleges did the same. However, just 12.5 percent of PhD-granting colleges and research universities went this route, as 37.5 percent of these participants adapted an open-source alternative. Where 33.33 percent of private schools programmed their own systems, just 19.05 percent of public schools did the same. Open-source alternatives were extremely popular among the largest schools in the sample (those with 15,000 or more students), as 53.85 percent of these participants adapted such a system. By comparison, the next closest enrollment range here was those schools with 2,500 to 7,499 students at 20 percent.

64.91 percent of libraries in the sample use a content management system for the library website, including 72.73 percent of community colleges and 69.23 percent of those colleges with 15,000 or more students. Whereas 66.67 percent of public schools in the sample use a CMS, 60 percent of private schools do. Among those participants that do use a CMS, the system used most often is Drupal, used by 32.43 percent of these participants. No participants reported using e107, TextPattern, or Zoop, and 2.7 percent of participants each reported using Joomla, Mambo, ModX, and Plone. 5.41 percent use WordPress. Drupal is not as popular with community colleges (used by 12.5 percent of participants that use a CMS) as it is with 4-year/MA-granting colleges (45.45 percent) or PhD-granting colleges and research universities (50 percent). It is also used more often among public schools (35.71 percent) than it is among private schools (22.22 percent).

Satisfaction with CMS

We asked survey participants to rate how satisfied they are with their current content management system. The majority are either "satisfied" (31.58 percent) or "quite satisfied" (29.82 percent), the highest two categories for this question. 10.53 percent say they are "not completely satisfied," while 14.04 percent plan to change systems. While the community colleges in the sample are the most likely to be changing systems (18.18 percent of them plan to do so), they are also the most satisfied with their current system as 68.18 percent are either "satisfied" or "quite satisfied"—57.9 percent of 4-year/MA-granting colleges and 56.25 percent of PhD-granting colleges and research universities can say the same.

Entering Content

In the last semester, a mean of 7.97 library personnel entered content into the college library websites of our participants. The median here was 3, while the range was from a low of 0 to a max of 100. PhD-granting colleges/research universities had by far the most personnel entering such data, with a mean of 18.87 doing so in the last semester (and a median of 6). The next closest were the 4-year/MA-granting colleges, with a mean of 5.94 and a median of 3.5, while community colleges had a mean of just 2.2 and a median of 1. No community college in the sample had more than 15 library personnel enter content onto the website. On average, public schools had more personnel entering content than private schools, a mean of 8.84 for the former and a mean of 5.67 for the latter. Aside from the one participant who responded with 100, only three other participants had more than 15 such personnel entering content onto the library website.

Consistency of Style and Brand Presentation

The majority of survey participants (73.68 percent) are "generally satisfied" with the consistency of style and brand presentation on the library's website. In fact, just 3.51 percent are "not very satisfied" in this department, while 1.75 percent do not consider this an important goal. 19.3 percent are "somewhat satisfied." Broken out by public and private status, the splits are nearly identical: 73.81 percent of the former are "generally satisfied," as are 73.33 percent of the latter. There is a little more variance when the data is broken out by full-time student enrollment, as 12.5 percent of those participants with less than 2,500 students are "not very satisfied" in this department, and just 56.25 percent are "generally satisfied." Compare this to those participants with 15,000 or more students, where 84.62 percent say they are "generally satisfied."

Ease of Applications within the CMS

We asked survey participants to rate the usability of a variety of actions and operations within the library's content management system.

Position and Manipulate Videos

22.81 percent of survey participants find it to be "relatively easy" to position and manipulate videos within the website's CMS, while an identical 22.81 percent find it to be "possible but with some restraints." 15.79 percent say it is "possible but with many restraints," while 10.53 percent say they are "not able to do" it. 14.04 percent say it is "very easy." Broken out by type of the college, the community colleges in the sample have the most difficulty with this, as 22.71 percent find it to be "possible but with many restraints" while another 22.73 percent say they are not able to do it at all. By comparison, just 10.52 percent of 4-year/MA-granting colleges rated these functions in either of these two categories, as did 18.75 percent of PhD-granting colleges and research universities. A quarter of all survey participants with less than 2,500 students say they are not able to do this either, with the next closest in this category belonging to those participants in the "7,500 to 14,999" enrollment range at 7.69 percent.

Enter the Same Content to Multiple Locations

19.3 percent of all survey participants say it is "very easy" to enter the same content to multiple locations on the site at the same time. However, 22.81 percent say they are not able to do it at all. 31.58 percent are evenly split between "relatively easy" and "possible but with some restraints," while 12.28 percent of participants say it is "possible but with many restraints." Again the community colleges have the most difficulty with these actions, as 50 percent of them say it is either "possible with buy many restraints" or that they are "not able to do" it. This is nearly double the percentages for both 4-year/MA-granting colleges (26.32 percent) and PhD-granting colleges/research universities (25 percent). The smallest schools (those with less than 2,500 students) also were the least satisfied with their ability to enter content to multiple locations on the site at the same time, as 18.75 percent say it is "possible but with many restraints" while 31.25 percent say this is something they are "not able to do."

Entering Charts, Tables, and Other Tabular Data

Just 8.77 percent of survey participants find it to be "very easy" to enter charts, tables, and other tabular data through the content management system, the lowest among all functions in this question. 45.62 percent are spilt evenly between "relatively easy" and "possible but with some restraints," while 19.3 percent rate the manipulation of these functions as "possible but with many restraints." 14.04 percent say they are not able to perform these functions, including 27.27 percent of community colleges. By comparison, no more than 6.25 percent of any other type of college rated these functions this way. Also, no community college rated this function as "very easy" to do, as compared to 21.05 percent of 4-year and MA-granting colleges. While a quarter of all survey participants with less than 2,500 students are not able to perform this function, this is true for just 7.69 percent of all participants in the "7,500 to 14,999" enrollment range as well as 7.69 percent of those in the "15,000 or more" range.

Check the Functionality of Page Links

31.58 percent of survey participants say it is "relatively easy" to check the functionality of page links and just 8.77 percent are not able to do this at all. Another 21.05 percent find it to be "very easy" to do, including 37.5 percent of PhD-granting colleges and research universities. While no community colleges are unable to check the functionality of page links, 27.27 percent do say it is only possible with many restraints. This ability is also less common with private schools than it is with public schools, as 26.67 percent of the former are unable to do so as compared to just 2.38 percent of the latter. Broken out by total full-time student enrollment, the participants in the "7,500 to 14,999" range are the most satisfied with their ability to check the functionality of pages links, as 38.46

percent of them find this to be "very easy," while this is the case for just 6.67 percent of participants in the "2,500 to 7,499" enrollment range.

Restricting Site Access

24.56 percent of all survey participants say they are able to restrict a large number of content providers to be able to access only very specific areas of the library's website, albeit with many restraints, while 22.81 percent say they are not able to do this at all. While 19.3 percent say this is "very easy," just 5.26 percent say it is "possible but with some restraints." Once again, the community colleges are the most likely not to be able to perform these functions, as 40.91 percent of them cite this to be the case. The next closest in this category are the PhD-granting colleges and research universities, where 12.5 percent of them are not able to do this. The larger schools have a much more success with this, as 38.46 percent of those in the "7,500 to 14,999" enrollment range and 46.15 percent of those in the "15,000 or more" enrollment range find these actions to be either "relatively easy" or "very easy" to perform. On the other end of the spectrum, 56.25 percent of survey participants with less than 2,500 students and 60 percent of those with 2,500 to 7,499 students are either not able to do this or find it to be "possible but with many restraints."

Provide a Report of Content Changes

35.09 percent of all survey participants are not able to produce a report of content changes for a specified period of time through the website's CMS, including 40.91 percent of community colleges, 46.67 percent of private schools, and more than 50 percent of those schools with less than 7,500 students. By comparison, 46.08 percent of schools with 7,500 or more students find this function to be either "relatively easy" or "very easy," as do 50 percent of all PhD-granting colleges and research universities.

PROGRAMMING

JacaScript is the most commonly used scripting language employed by the libraries in the sample, used by nearly half (47.37 percent) of all participants. The next closest was PHP (17.54 percent), while 5.26 percent of libraries in the sample use Perl and 1.75 percent use CGI. 7.02 percent of participants use a scripting language not listed in the question. Broken out by type of college, JavaScript is heavily preferred by community colleges (59.09 percent) and 4-year/MA-granting colleges (52.63 percent), while just 25 percent of the PhD-granting colleges and research universities in the sample use this language. Alternatively, 31.25 percent of libraries at these institutions use PHP, while 18.75 percent use Perl, the only type of college that employs this language. JavaScript is also favored more heavily by the smaller schools than it is the larger schools: 56.25 percent of libraries at schools with enrollments under 2,500, as well as 60 percent of those in the "2,500 to 7,499" enrollment range, employ JavaScript, as compared to just

30.77 percent of those in the "7,500 to 14,999" employment range and 38.46 percent of those with 15,000 or more students.

Who Does the Script Work?

We asked survey participants approximately what percentage of the total script work is done by each of the following sources: library IT personnel; MLS librarians; college administration IT personnel; or outside consultants and freelancers.

MLS Librarians

For the most part, the greatest amount of script work is performed by MLS librarians, as survey participants say this group handles the script work a mean of 43.62 percent of the time. Aside from having the highest mean, MLS librarians are also the only group with a median other than 0 percent (the median here is 7.5 percent). These MLS librarians are preferred by 4-year/MA-granting colleges, as they perform these duties a mean of 65 percent of the time. This category also posts a median of 97.5 percent. By comparison, the next highest mean when broken out by type of college belongs to the PhD-granting colleges and research universities at 36.73 percent, and the next closest median is 1 percent. There is not much difference between public (mean of 42.33 percent) and private schools here (48.33 percent), although there is a significant divergence when the data is broken out by full-time student enrollment: for those in the "2,500 to 7,499" enrollment group the mean is 57.27 percent, and for those in the "7,500 to 14,999" enrollment range the mean is 59 percent, yet this figure drops dramatically to 17.67 percent for the top tier libraries in this category (those at schools with 15,000 or more students).

Library and College administration IT Personnel

The next group of workers most employed to perform the script work for the library website are the library IT personnel (they do so a mean of 30 percent of the time) and the college administration IT personnel (mean of 26.43 percent). Both groups have medians of 0 percent. Broken out by type of college, the PhD-granting colleges and research universities are much more likely than the rest to use the former group for this work, doing so a mean of 53.27 percent of the time, while the community colleges in the sample much prefer to use the college administration IT department, using that group a mean of 47.67 percent of the time. By comparison, the next closest mean for either group of workers is 19.83 percent, posted by the 4-year/MA-granting colleges using the college IT department. Broken out by public and private status, there isn't much of a split for those participants using the college IT department for this work (a mean of 25.55 percent for the former, 29.67 percent for the latter), although the split for those participants using library IT personnel for script work is sizable, as the former uses these workers a mean of 32.58 percent of the time while the latter uses them a mean of 20.56 percent. One last oddity appears when the data is broken out by full-time student enrollment, as those libraries at schools with 15,000 or more students employ library IT personnel for the library website's script work a mean of 59.42 percent of the time, whereas the next closest mean in this category belongs to the "7,500 to 14,999" enrollment range with a mean of 26 percent.

Outside Consultants and Freelancers

The libraries in the sample use outside consultants and freelancers for just a mean of 2.33 percent of the script work for the library website.

Cascading Style Sheets

64.91 percent of libraries in the sample use Cascading Style Sheets "extensively," while another 19.3 percent use them "moderately." Just 7.02 percent do not use them at all. Community colleges are the most hesitant in this respect, as just 40.91 percent of these colleges use them extensively, compared to 73.68 percent of 4-year/MA-granting colleges and 87.5 percent of PhD-granting colleges and research universities. Public schools might also be considered a step behind here, with just 61.9 percent of them using Cascading Style Sheets extensively while 73.33 percent of private schools use them this way. However, just 4.76 percent of the former do not use them at all, compared to 13.33 percent of the latter. Considering the entire sample, all those participants that do not use Cascading Style Sheets at all are schools with less than 7,500 students, while those in the "7,500 to 14,999" enrollment range use them extensively 76.92 percent of the time, as do 92.31 percent of those with 15,000 or more students.

Embedded Styles

A mean of 25.54 percent of the Cascading Style Styles used by the libraries in the sample are in the "embedded styles" format. The median here is 10 percent, and the range is from 0 to 100 percent. Community colleges use the embedded styles format the least, a mean of just 7.28 percent of the time, while the means for the two remaining types of colleges are 3-5 times greater. In fact, no community college uses embedded styles for more than 25 percent of their Cascading Style Sheets. The smallest schools (those with less than 2,500 students) are the most likely to use this format, as it is used a mean of 41.06 percent of the time. The next closest mean in this category belongs to the "7,500 to 14,999"enrollment range at 25.3 percent.

Dynamic, Database-driven Web Pages

According to our survey participants, a mean of 31.26 percent of the routine content updates for the library website are done through dynamic, database-driven web pages rather than through static pages. This figure is much higher for PhD-granting colleges and research universities (47.81 percent) than it is for community colleges (15.79

percent). Broken out by public and private status, the split isn't quite so drastic: a mean of 29.64 percent for the former, and a mean of 35.58 percent for the latter. For those libraries at schools with less than 15,000 students, the means are between 20 and 29 percent, but this mean jumps dramatically for the highest tier in this category (15,000 or more students), up to a mean of 48.08 percent. This group also posts the highest median at 25 percent.

Social Bookmarking

We asked survey participants if the library website maintains an internal social bookmarking list or utilizes an external bookmarking software or service (or else provide links to such a service). 24.56 percent of participants say the library provides links on the website to a social bookmarking software or service, by far the most among respondents. However, the majority of participants (68.42 percent) did not answer this question.

Mashups by Library Staff

87.72 percent of survey participants do not offer mashups devised by library staff via the library website. This figure remains fairly constant across the board when the data is broken out by type of college (between 86 and 90 percent), although the gap widens somewhat when broken out by public or private status: 85.71 percent of the former do not offer these mashups, as compared to 93.33 percent of the latter. The lone anomaly in the full-time enrollment category occurs in the "7,500 to 14,999" range, where 92.31 percent of libraries in the sample do not offer mashups on the library website devised by library staff. By comparison, all other ranges in this category are between 84.5 and 87.5 percent.

Mashups by Others

Even fewer survey participants offer links to mashups devised by non-staff members: just 7.02 percent of the sample. The PhD-granting colleges and research universities are the most likely, as 12.5 percent of them do, compared to just 4.55 percent of community colleges and 5.26 percent of 4-year/MA-granting colleges. Whereas no private schools offer these kinds of mashups, 9.52 percent of public schools in the sample do. Again an anomaly occurs in the full-time enrollment category, as 15.38 percent of those libraries in the "7,500 to 14,999" range offer mashups devised by others, or twice the percentage of the next highest in this category.

FEDERATED SEARCH

Handling of Federated Search

The majority of survey participants (63.16 percent) use a commercial discovery platform when it comes to federated search, while a sizeable amount (33.33 percent) do not emphasize federated search at all. Just one library in the sample has devised its own federated search engine. 40.91 percent of community colleges do not emphasize federated search, nor do 53.33 percent of participants with enrollments between 2,500 and 7,499.

WEBSITE MARKETING

Social Media

We asked survey participants if the library has a presence on any of the following social networking or file-sharing sites: Twitter; Pinterest; YouTube; Vimeo; or Facebook.

Twitter and YouTube

Twitter and YouTube proved to be quite popular, as 56.14 percent of survey participants cited a presence on Twitter and 50.88 percent have a presence on YouTube. In both instances, the PhD-granting colleges and research universities have the greatest presence among all types of colleges in the sample, as 68.75 percent are on Twitter and 56.25 percent are on YouTube. Compare this to community colleges, where 45.45 percent are on the former and an identical 45.45 percent are on the latter. There is a great gulf between public schools and private schools here: 61.9 percent of public schools have a presence on Twitter, while just 40 percent of the private schools in the sample can say the same. Even more drastic is the split for those libraries with a presence on YouTube, with a similar 61.9 percent of public schools having such a presence yet just 20 percent of private schools are on the video-sharing site. Broken out by full-time student enrollment, we find that every survey participant with at least 15,000 students has a presence on Twitter (while all other categories in this breakout range from 40 to 47 percent). Similarly, but not quite as drastically, are the results for YouTube: 76.92 percent of all those participants at schools with 7,500 or more students have a presence on YouTube, while no more than 40 percent of all other sized schools can say the same.

Facebook

However, the most popular among the social media sites is Facebook, with 80.7 percent of all survey participants saying the library has a presence on the site, including 94.74 percent of 4-year/MA-granting colleges, 93.75 percent of PhD-granting colleges and research universities, and 86.67 percent of private schools. Community colleges lag behind at just 59.09 percent. 100 percent of the libraries in the sample at schools with 15,000 or more students have a Facebook presence, although only 68.75 percent of those with less than 2,500 students are on the popular social networking site, as are just 73.33 percent of those in the "2,500 to 7,499" enrollment range.

Pinterest and Vimeo

Nearly a quarter (24.56 percent) of survey participants are on the site Pinterest. The split between public and private is fairly even (23.81 percent for the former, 26.67 percent for the latter), although when broken out by type of college the data shows that community colleges are less than likely to be on the site, as just 18.18 percent of them are. Compare this to 4-year and MA-granting colleges, where 31.58 percent maintain a presence on Pinterest. An interesting anomaly appears in the full-time student enrollment category, as 38.46 percent of those in the "15,000 or more" range are on Pinterest as well as 25 percent of those in the "less than 2,500" range, and yet only 13.33 percent of those in the "2,500 to 7,499" range can say the same.

Just 7.02 percent of all survey particpants are on the video-sharing site Vimeo, none of which are community colleges. While this figure is higher for private schools (13.33 percent), public schools are less than likely to be on the site (4.76 percent). Of note is that 12. 5 percent of those participants with enrollments under 2,500 say they maintain a presence on Vimeo.

Use of Blogs

Just more than half (54.39 percent) of all survey participants maintain at least one blog for the benefit of those patrons who want to keep up with library news. These are much more common among PhD-granting colleges and research universities (75 percent) than they are with community colleges (45.45 percent) or 4-year/MA-granting colleges (47.37 percent). There is also a great gap between public schools and private schools, as 59.52 percent of the former maintain such blogs while just 40 percent of the latter can say the same. As full-time student enrollment increases, so too does the prevalence of these blogs: while just 31.25 percent of participants with less than 2,500 students maintain blogs for these purposes, this figure jumps to 53.33 for the next enrollment range (2,500 to 7,499 students). What's more, this figure rises to 69.23 percent for all participants with at least 7,500 students.

Use of RSS Feeds and Email Newsletters

After blogs, the most popular ways of keeping library patrons up to date with library news are RSS feeds (used by 42.11 percent of survey participants) and email newsletters (31.58 percent). Both of these are favored by PhD-granting colleges and research universities, as 68.75 percent of them use RSS feeds and an identical 68.75 percent use email newsletters, the most by any type of college. Of note is that only 27.27 percent of community colleges in the sample use RSS feeds, and just 9.09 percent of these same participants use email newsletters. 4-year and MA-granting colleges, too, fall below the average here: 36.84 percent use the former, 26.32 percent use the latter. Public schools are much more likely to use RSS feeds than private schools (52.38 percent to 13.33 percent), while the reverse is true for email newsletters (used by 28.57 percent of public schools and 40 percent of private). In both cases, however, the larger schools employ these techniques more often than their smaller counterparts: among those schools with less than 2,500 students, 12.5 percent maintain email newsletters, while 18.75 percent have RSS feeds. These figures rise consistently and without waiver as student enrollment increases, culminating at 53.85 percent for the former and 76.92 percent for the latter in the "15,000 or more" enrollment range.

Use of Listservs and Podcasts

Listservs and podcasts prove to be much less popular means of keeping library patrons up to date on library news, as only four survey participants (7.02 percent of the sample) maintain listservs for these purposes and just one participant has a podcast. Of those four participants that maintain listservs, just one is a public school and none are community colleges. The lone participant with a podcast is a public PhD-granting college or research university with 15,000 or more students.

Number of RSS Feeds

The libraries in the sample have a mean of 6 separate RSS feeds or electronic newsletters about the library and its services that can be subscribed to via the library website. The median, however, is 1, as the overall mean is greatly offset by one participant's response of 126. In fact, no other survey participant has more than 40 such RSS feeds available, while 18 do not have any. Community colleges have the most, a mean of 9.5 (again aided greatly by the one response of 126), while 4-year/MA-granting colleges have a mean of just 1.43. All three types of colleges in the sample posted a median of 1. Public schools have a mean of 7.67 RSS feeds and a median of 1, while private schools have a mean of 1.42 and a median of 0. As full-time student enrollment increases, there is a clear increase in the number of RSS feeds of our participants: from a mean of 0.38 for the smallest schools (less than 2,500 students), up to a mean of 1.67 for those in the "2,500 to 7,499" range, a mean of 5.44 in the "7,500 to 14,999" range, and finally all the way up to 17.82 for those schools with 15,000 or more students.

Subscribers to RSS Feeds

The mean number of total subscribers to these RSS feeds is 29.17, although the median is 0. While one participant cites 500 such subscribers, and another has 150, no other libraries in the sample have more than 20 subscribers to their RSS feeds. The one participant with 500 subscribers is a public 4-year/MA-granting college with 2,500 to

7,499 students. No private school cites more than 2 subscribers, and no PhD-granting college or research university has more than 9.

Customization to the Library Website

Just 19.3 percent of libraries in the sample say their website includes personal customization features that enable end users to construct their own personal "my Library" identity, enabling users to save research strategies, favorite places, and/or other commonly used library resources—although another 7.02 percent of libraries are planning on adding this but have not done so yet. These customizations are more common with community colleges, where 27.27 percent of participants say they have such features, as compared to 4-year/MA-granting colleges (15.79 percent) and PhD-granting colleges and research universities (12.5 percent). No private schools in the sample currently have such features in place, while 26.19 percent of public schools in the sample do.

Search Engine Optimization

The libraries in the sample spend a mean of 8.61 hours per month on search engine optimization for the library website. The median, however, is 0. The maximum is 140, cited by a public PhD-granting college or research university with 2,500 to 7,499 students. Community colleges spend a mean of 2.18 hours per month in this fashion, while 4-year/MA-granting colleges spend a mean of 5.67 hours. Both have medians of 0, however. Broken out by public and private status, the public schools spend a mean of 5.85 hours on SEO per month, while private schools spent more than three times the amount of time on this, a mean of 18.8 hours/month. Interestingly, those schools in the "2,500 to 7,499" student enrollment range spend the most time with this, a mean of 23.54 hours per month. By comparison, no other library in the sample spends more than 25 hours this way, and no other range in this category has a mean higher than 6.17.

Updating Social Media

A mean of 12.04 hours per month is spent by survey participants updating the library's presence on Facebook, Twitter, YouTube, Pinterest, Vimeo, and other such social media sites. The median is 7 hours, and the maximum is 100. Broken out by type of college, the means are fairly consistent, from a low of 10.06 for community colleges to a high of 13.59 for the 4-year/MA-granting colleges. The same can be said for the split between public and private: 11.43 for the former, 13.77 for the latter. However, there are some anomalies when the data is broken out by full-time student enrollment, as the mean for both the smallest and largest enrollment groups here are 17.54 hours, while the means for the two middle ranges are between 5.5 and 7.5.

REDESIGN

Within the past year, 43.86 percent of survey participants have launched any kind of major website redesign, including 62.5 percent of PhD-granting colleges and research universities and 61.54 percent of those libraries at schools with 15,000 or more students. Only 36.36 percent of community colleges in the sample launched a website redesign in the last year, as did just 36.84 percent of 4-year/MA-granting colleges. Public schools (47.62 percent) were more likely than private schools (33.33 percent) to have done this. Only 31.25 percent of those participants with less than 2,500 full-time enrolled students have redesigned in the past year.

However, 56.14 percent of all survey participants do plan a major redesign of the library website within the next two years, including 68.75 percent of PhD-granting colleges and research universities and 84.62 percent of schools with enrolments of 15,000 or more— the same participants that were most likely to have redesigned within the past year. The split between public and private schools in the sample is fairly even: 57.14 percent for the former, 53.33 percent for the latter. More community colleges will redesign within the next two years than have redesigned within the past year, as 45.45 percent of them have plans to do so. Still, for the smallest schools (less than 2,500 students), the likelihood of a redesign in the future is less than favorable, as just 37.5 percent of these libraries plan on doing so.

LIBRARY WEBSITE BUDGET

Where Does the Library Website Budget Come From?

For more than half (56.14 percent) of all survey participants, the library website's budget is part of the library IT budget, while a third of participants say the website budget is a part of the college IT budget. Just one participant cites it to be a separate line item in the overall library budget. Broken out by type of college, the PhD-granting colleges and research universities are most likely to have the library website budget as a party of the library IT budget as 68.75 percent of them do, compared to 57.89 percent of 4-year/MA-granting colleges and 45.45 percent of community colleges. There is an even greater gulf when the data is broken out by public and private status: 64.29 percent of the former cite the budget to be a part of the library IT budget, while just 33.33 percent of the latter say the same. While all survey participants with less than 15,000 students report this to be the case 46-53 percent of the time, 76.92 percent of those libraries at schools with 15,000 or more students say this is so.

How Much is the Library Website Budget?

The libraries in the sample report that the annual central budget for the library website constitutes a mean of $10,670. However, this mean is greatly offset by one response of

$100,000, as the median is $0. More accurately, only seven libraries in the sample have a budget of $10,000 or more for the library website. The community colleges have the lowest mean here at $3,270, while the mean for 4-year/MA-granting colleges is $13,800 and the mean of PhD-granting colleges and research universities is $20,222. Still, the median for all three types of colleges is $0. Broken out by public and private, the public schools have the greater mean ($11,286 to $6,363), although the private schools have a great median ($225 to $0). The one respondent with a library website budget of $100,000 per year is a public PhD-granting college/research university with 15,000 or more students. Interestingly, the mean for those libraries in the sample in the "2,500 to 7,499" enrollment range is just $50 as no participant here allocates more than $400 to this respect. Many libraries do not appear to have a line item in the budget for the library website but spending is likely spread over other categories.

Change in Spending

Total spending on the college library websites of our survey participants has increased by a mean of 2.71 percent in the past year. The most it has increased is by 50 percent, while one participant says it has decreased by 20 percent. The median for the entire sample is 0 percent (no change). Community colleges are the only type of colleges in the sample that report the spending in this respect has decreased in the past year (by a mean of 1.32 percent). Those schools with less than 2,500 students also say their spending has decreased over this time, a mean of 3.3 percent. PhD-granting colleges and research universities say it has increased by a mean of 7 percent, and those schools with 15,000 or more students posted a mean increase of 7.5 percent. Broken out by public and private status, the public schools cite an increase of a mean of 2.4 percent, while private schools cite a mean increase of 4.63 percent.

Survey participants do not expect this to change much over the next year, as they expect a mean of just a 1 percent increase in spending on the library budget over this time. While two participants do expect spending to decrease by 20 percent (both of them community colleges with less than 2,500 students), the majority of libraries in the sample do not expect it to change at all, resulting in a median of 0 percent. The high here is an expected 25 percent increase.

Spending on Freelancers and Outside Programmers

The libraries in the sample spent a mean of $2,612 for outside programmers, consultants, and freelancers to alter, upgrade, or service in any way the library website. This mean was greatly affected by two participants' responses of $40,000 and $50,000. Indeed, the overall sample median was $0, and 35 of 42 respondents to this question cited spending nothing in this respect. The two participants who spent $40,000 and $50,000 were a 4-year/MA-granting college and a PhD-granting college/research university, respectively, one public (the latter) and one private (the former). On average, the private schools outspend the public schools to this end, with a mean of $6,286 compared to $1,877.

No libraries in the sample spent anything in the last three years for freelancers or consultants to update or upgrade the library's social media sites.

WEB STATISTICS

Files on the Web Site

According to our survey participants, the library web site contains a mean of 1,219 files. The median here is 500, while the range is from 10 to 10,000. On average, the PhD-granting colleges and research universities have the most files on the library website, a mean of 1,508, while the community colleges have the least, a mean of 908. The split between public (a mean of 1,108) and private (mean of 1,567) is closer than this, although there is a great discrepancy when the data is broken out by full-time student enrollment: the high mean in this category belongs to the "2,500 to 7,499" enrollment range, with a mean of 2,090 files, while the low here is a mean of 188 for those libraries at schools with less than 2,500 students. The two remaining enrollment ranges lie somewhere in the middle, with means of 1,010 and 1,276.

Unique Visitors

The libraries in the sample average 50,109 weekly unique visitors to the library website from September through May. The median here is 8,000 visitors, while the maximum is 950,887. This maximum was reported by a community college, thus skyrocketing the category's mean to 141,662, although both 4-year/MA-granting colleges and PhD-granting colleges and research universities posted higher medians (7,500 and 10,000, respectively). This high response also inflated the mean for the public schools in the sample, up to 64,764 unique visitors per week, while the private schools average just 4,312 in that same time. Public schools also outpaced the private schools in terms of median, 8,531 to 2,800.

Chapter 1: College Library Web Staff

Table 1.1: Does the college library have its own webmaster or web staff that is separate from the college website staff?

	No Answer	Yes	No
Entire sample	0.00%	61.40%	38.60%

Table 1.2: Does the college library have its own webmaster or web staff that is separate from the college website staff? Broken out by type of college.

Type of College	Yes	No
Community college	36.36%	63.64%
4-year/MA-granting college	73.68%	26.32%
PhD-granting college/Research university	81.25%	18.75%

Table 1.3: Does the college library have its own webmaster or web staff that is separate from the college website staff? Broken out by public or private status of the college.

Public or Private	Yes	No
Public	61.90%	38.10%
Private	60.00%	40.00%

Table 1.4: Does the college library have its own webmaster or web staff that is separate from the college website staff? Broken out by full-time equivalent student enrollment of the college.

Enrollment	Yes	No
Less than 2,500	37.50%	62.50%
2,500 to 7,499	60.00%	40.00%
7,500 to 14,999	69.23%	30.77%
15,000 or more	84.62%	15.38%

Table 1.5: If the college does not have a separate webmaster or web staff, who runs the library website?

	Library IT staff	Library administration	Central college website staff
Entire sample	52.38%	28.57%	19.05%

Table 1.6: If the college does not have a separate webmaster or web staff, who runs the library website? Broken out by type of college.

Type of College	Library IT staff	Library administration	Central college website staff
Community college	46.15%	30.77%	23.08%
4-year/MA-granting college	60.00%	20.00%	20.00%
PhD-granting college/Research university	66.67%	33.33%	0.00%

Table 1.7: If the college does not have a separate webmaster or web staff, who runs the library website? Broken out by public or private status of the college.

Public or Private	Library IT staff	Library administration	Central college website staff
Public	53.33%	26.67%	20.00%
Private	50.00%	33.33%	16.67%

Table 1.8: If the college does not have a separate webmaster or web staff, who runs the library website? Broken out by full-time equivalent student enrollment of the college.

Enrollment	Library IT staff	Library administration	Central college website staff
Less than 2,500	33.33%	33.33%	33.33%
2,500 to 7,499	66.67%	16.67%	16.67%
7,500 to 14,999	75.00%	25.00%	0.00%
15,000 or more	50.00%	50.00%	0.00%

Table 1.9: What percentage of the total man hours spent in running the college library website are provided by the following?

Table 1.9A: College-wide web or Information Technology staff

	Mean	Median	Minimum	Maximum
Entire sample	14.70%	0.00%	0.00%	100.00%

Table 1.9B: Library web or Information Technology staff

	Mean	Median	Minimum	Maximum
Entire sample	83.00%	99.00%	0.00%	100.00%

Table 1.9C: Consultants, outsourced service providers, or other third parties

	Mean	Median	Minimum	Maximum
Entire sample	2.25%	0.00%	0.00%	100.00%

Table 1.10: What percentage of the total man hours spent in running the college library website are provided by the following? Broken out by type of college.

Table 1.10A: College-wide web or Information Technology staff

Type of College	Mean	Median	Minimum	Maximum
Community college	28.90%	10.00%	0.00%	100.00%
4-year/MA-granting college	5.69%	0.00%	0.00%	30.00%
PhD-granting college/Research university	5.06%	0.00%	0.00%	50.00%

Table 1.10B: Library web or Information Technology staff

Type of College	Mean	Median	Minimum	Maximum
Community college	70.62%	90.00%	0.00%	100.00%
4-year/MA-granting college	88.00%	99.00%	0.00%	100.00%
PhD-granting college/Research university	94.25%	100.00%	50.00%	100.00%

Table 1.10C: Consultants, outsourced service providers, or other third parties

Type of College	Mean	Median	Minimum	Maximum
Community college	0.25%	0.00%	0.00%	5.00%
4-year/MA-granting college	6.31%	0.00%	0.00%	100.00%
PhD-granting college/Research university	0.69%	0.00%	0.00%	10.00%

Table 1.11: What percentage of the total man hours spent in running the college library website are provided by the following? Broken out by public or private status of the college.

Table 1.11A: College-wide web or Information Technology staff

Public or Private	Mean	Median	Minimum	Maximum
Public	17.64%	2.00%	0.00%	100.00%
Private	6.50%	0.00%	0.00%	40.00%

Table 1.11B: Library web or Information Technology staff

Public or Private	Mean	Median	Minimum	Maximum
Public	82.05%	95.00%	0.00%	100.00%
Private	85.64%	100.00%	0.00%	100.00%

Table 1.11C: Consultants, outsourced service providers, or other third parties

Public or Private	Mean	Median	Minimum	Maximum
Public	0.18%	0.00%	0.00%	5.00%
Private	7.86%	0.00%	0.00%	100.00%

Table 1.12: What percentage of the total man hours spent in running the college library website are provided by the following? Broken out by full-time equivalent student enrollment of the college.

Table 1.12A: College-wide web or Information Technology staff

Enrollment	Mean	Median	Minimum	Maximum
Less than 2,500	24.20%	5.00%	0.00%	100.00%
2,500 to 7,499	12.86%	2.50%	0.00%	80.00%
7,500 to 14,999	15.45%	0.00%	0.00%	75.00%
15,000 or more	5.08%	0.00%	0.00%	40.00%

Table 1.12B: Library web staff or Information Technology staff

Enrollment	Mean	Median	Minimum	Maximum
Less than 2,500	68.47%	90.00%	0.00%	100.00%
2,500 to 7,499	87.14%	97.50%	20.00%	100.00%
7,500 to 14,999	84.00%	99.00%	25.00%	100.00%
15,000 or more	94.46%	100.00%	60.00%	100.00%

Table 1.12C: Consultants, outsourced service providers, or other third parties

Enrollment	Mean	Median	Minimum	Maximum
Less than 2,500	7.33%	0.00%	0.00%	100.00%
2,500 to 7,499	0.00%	0.00%	0.00%	0.00%
7,500 to 14,999	0.10%	0.00%	0.00%	1.00%
15,000 or more	0.46%	0.00%	0.00%	5.00%

Table 1.13: How many full-time equivalent library staff positions are devoted to the technological aspects of running the library website?

	Mean	Median	Minimum	Maximum
Entire sample	1.42	1.00	0.00	20.00

Table 1.14: How many full-time equivalent library staff positions are devoted to the technological aspects of running the library website? Broken out by type of college.

Type of College	Mean	Median	Minimum	Maximum
Community college	0.71	0.50	0.00	5.00
4-year/MA-granting college	1.16	1.00	0.10	3.00
PhD-granting college/Research university	2.66	1.00	0.25	20.00

Table 1.15: How many full-time equivalent library staff positions are devoted to the technological aspects of running the library website? Broken out by public or private status of the college.

Public or Private	Mean	Median	Minimum	Maximum
Public	1.39	1.00	0.00	20.00
Private	1.48	1.00	0.05	5.00

Table 1.16: How many full-time equivalent library staff positions are devoted to the technological aspects of running the library website? Broken out by full-time equivalent student enrollment of the college.

Enrollment	Mean	Median	Minimum	Maximum
Less than 2,500	1.08	0.75	0.10	5.00
2,500 to 7,499	1.00	1.00	0.00	4.00
7,500 to 14,999	0.96	1.00	0.25	3.00
15,000 or more	2.71	1.00	0.25	20.00

Table 1.17: How is the library website handled on a day-to-day basis?

	No Answer	College IT staff does most technical work and the library handles content	Library IT staff does most technical work and the library handles content
Entire sample	0.00%	33.33%	66.67%

Table 1.18: How is the library website handled on a day-to-day basis? Broken out by type of college.

Type of College	College IT staff does most technical work and the library handles content	Library IT staff does most technical work and the library handles content
Community college	50.00%	50.00%
4-year/MA-granting college	31.58%	68.42%
PhD-granting college/Research university	12.50%	87.50%

Table 1.19: How is the library website handled on a day-to-day basis? Broken out by public or private status of the college.

Public or Private	College IT staff does most technical work and the library handles content	Library IT staff does most technical work and the library handles content
Public	35.71%	64.29%
Private	26.67%	73.33%

Table 1.20: How is the library website handled on a day-to-day basis? Broken out by full-time equivalent student enrollment of the college.

Enrollment	College IT staff does most technical work and the library handles content	Library IT staff does most technical work and the library handles content
Less than 2,500	43.75%	56.25%
2,500 to 7,499	33.33%	66.67%
7,500 to 14,999	38.46%	61.54%
15,000 or more	15.38%	84.62%

Table 1.21: Which phrase best describes your library's web team?

	We do some content editing but don't have a full-time webmaster	We have a webmaster and a little bit of help from others	We have a webmaster plus a small staff of 2-5 FTE positions	We have a webmaster plus a staff of more than 5 FTE positions	More than one webmaster for more than one website
Entire sample	29.09%	52.73%	16.36%	0.00%	1.82%

Table 1.22: Which phrase best describes your library's web team? Broken out by type of college.

Type of College	We do some content editing but don't have a full-time webmaster	We have a webmaster and a little bit of help from others	We have a webmaster plus a small staff of 2-5 FTE positions	We have a webmaster plus a staff of more than 5 FTE positions	More than one webmaster for more than one website
Community college	50.00%	36.36%	9.09%	0.00%	4.55%
4-year/MA-granting college	16.67%	72.22%	11.11%	0.00%	0.00%
PhD-granting college/Research university	13.33%	53.33%	33.33%	0.00%	0.00%

Table 1.23: Which phrase best describes your library's web team? Broken out by public or private status of the college.

Public or Private	We do some content editing but don't have a full-time webmaster	We have a webmaster and a little bit of help from others	We have a webmaster plus a small staff of 2-5 FTE positions	We have a webmaster plus a staff of more than 5 FTE positions	More than one webmaster for more than one website
Public	29.27%	53.66%	17.07%	0.00%	0.00%
Private	28.57%	50.00%	14.29%	0.00%	7.14%

Table 1.24: Which phrase best describes your library's web team? Broken out by full-time equivalent student enrollment of the college.

Enrollment	We do some content editing but don't have a full-time webmaster	We have a webmaster and a little bit of help from others	We have a webmaster plus a small staff of 2-5 FTE positions	We have a webmaster plus a staff of more than 5 FTE positions	More than one webmaster for more than one website
Less than 2,500	46.67%	53.33%	0.00%	0.00%	0.00%
2,500 to 7,499	20.00%	53.33%	20.00%	0.00%	6.67%
7,500 to 14,999	30.77%	61.54%	7.69%	0.00%	0.00%
15,000 or more	16.67%	41.67%	41.67%	0.00%	0.00%

Table 1.25: How many of each of the following does the library have for the internal communications needs of librarians or others who work for or with the library?

Table 1.25A: Listservs

	Mean	Median	Minimum	Maximum
Entire sample	4.67	0.00	0.00	100.00

Table 1.25B: Blogs

	Mean	Median	Minimum	Maximum
Entire sample	1.00	0.00	0.00	25.00

Table 1.25C: eNewsletter

	Mean	Median	Minimum	Maximum
Entire sample	0.19	0.00	0.00	1.00

Table 1.26: How many of each of the following does the library have for the internal communications needs of librarians or others who work for or with the library? Broken out by type of college.

Table 1.26A: Listservs

Type of College	Mean	Median	Minimum	Maximum
Community college	0.63	0.00	0.00	10.00
4-year/MA-granting college	1.25	0.00	0.00	10.00
PhD-granting college/Research university	11.73	0.00	0.00	100.00

Table 1.26B: Blogs

Type of College	Mean	Median	Minimum	Maximum
Community college	0.31	0.00	0.00	1.00
4-year/MA-granting college	0.58	0.50	0.00	2.00
PhD-granting college/Research university	2.07	0.00	0.00	25.00

Table 1.26C: eNewsletter

Type of College	Mean	Median	Minimum	Maximum
Community college	0.00	0.00	0.00	0.00
4-year/MA-granting college	0.25	0.00	0.00	1.00
PhD-granting college/Research university	0.33	0.00	0.00	1.00

Table 1.27: How many of each of the following does the library have for the internal communications needs of librarians or others who work for or with the library? Broken out by public or private status of the college.

Table 1.27A: Listservs

Public or Private	Mean	Median	Minimum	Maximum
Public	5.29	0.00	0.00	100.00
Private	2.33	0.00	0.00	20.00

Table 1.27B: Blogs

Public or Private	Mean	Median	Minimum	Maximum
Public	1.15	0.00	0.00	25.00
Private	0.44	0.00	0.00	1.00

Table 1.27C: eNewsletter

Public or Private	Mean	Median	Minimum	Maximum
Public	0.18	0.00	0.00	1.00
Private	0.22	0.00	0.00	1.00

Table 1.28: How many of each of the following does the library have for the internal communications needs of librarians or others who work for or with the library? Broken out by full-time equivalent student enrollment of the college.

Table 1.28A: Listservs

Enrollment	Mean	Median	Minimum	Maximum
Less than 2,500	0.30	0.00	0.00	3.00
2,500 to 7,499	2.20	0.00	0.00	20.00
7,500 to 14,999	1.00	0.00	0.00	10.00
15,000 or more	13.75	0.00	0.00	100.00

Table 1.28B: Blogs

Enrollment	Mean	Median	Minimum	Maximum
Less than 2,500	0.30	0.00	0.00	1.00
2,500 to 7,499	0.30	0.00	0.00	1.00
7,500 to 14,999	0.45	0.00	0.00	2.00
15,000 or more	2.67	1.00	0.00	25.00

Table 1.28C: eNewsletter

Enrollment	Mean	Median	Minimum	Maximum
Less than 2,500	0.00	0.00	0.00	0.00
2,500 to 7,499	0.30	0.00	0.00	1.00
7,500 to 14,999	0.18	0.00	0.00	1.00
15,000 or more	0.25	0.00	0.00	1.00

Table 1.29: Approximately how many people outside your central library web staff typically enter page content in a given semester?

	Mean	Median	Minimum	Maximum
Entire sample	6.79	0.00	0.00	100.00

Table 1.30: Approximately how many people outside your central library web staff typically enter page content in a given semester? Broken out by type of college.

Type of College	Mean	Median	Minimum	Maximum
Community college	1.35	0.00	0.00	12.00
4-year/MA-granting college	3.29	0.00	0.00	32.00
PhD-granting college/Research university	18.00	4.00	0.00	100.00

Table 1.31: Approximately how many people outside your central library web staff typically enter page content in a given semester? Broken out by public or private status of the college.

Public or Private	Mean	Median	Minimum	Maximum
Public	7.97	0.00	0.00	100.00
Private	3.23	0.00	0.00	30.00

Table 1.32: Approximately how many people outside your central library web staff typically enter page content in a given semester? Broken out by full-time equivalent student enrollment of the college.

Enrollment	Mean	Median	Minimum	Maximum
Less than 2,500	1.23	1.00	0.00	6.00
2,500 to 7,499	3.43	0.00	0.00	30.00
7,500 to 14,999	2.92	0.00	0.00	32.00
15,000 or more	20.88	7.50	0.00	100.00

Table 1.33: If the library has one or more committees to oversee website policy in any respect (content, IT, graphics, etc.), how many total individuals sit on these committees?

	Mean	Median	Minimum	Maximum
Entire sample	7.08	6.00	1.00	20.00

Table 1.34: If the library has one or more committees to oversee website policy in any respect (content, IT, graphics, etc.), how many total individuals sit on these committees? Broken out by type of college.

Type of College	Mean	Median	Minimum	Maximum
Community college	5.86	6.00	1.00	10.00
4-year/MA-granting college	7.00	5.50	4.00	18.00
PhD-granting college/Research university	7.91	6.00	5.00	20.00

Table 1.35: If the library has one or more committees to oversee website policy in any respect (content, IT, graphics, etc.), how many total individuals sit on these committees? Broken out by public or private status of the college.

Public or Private	Mean	Median	Minimum	Maximum
Public	7.36	6.00	1.00	20.00
Private	5.50	5.50	4.00	7.00

Table 1.36: If the library has one or more committees to oversee website policy in any respect (content, IT, graphics, etc.), how many total individuals sit on these committees? Broken out by full-time equivalent student enrollment of the college.

Enrollment	Mean	Median	Minimum	Maximum
Less than 2,500	6.00	6.00	4.00	8.00
2,500 to 7,499	6.13	5.00	1.00	18.00
7,500 to 14,999	6.33	7.00	5.00	7.00
15,000 or more	8.17	6.50	5.00	20.00

Describe the relationship between those at the library who run the website and those who may run library-related media sites on Facebook, YouTube, Pinterest, and other social media sites. Are they more or less run by the same parties? Are the staffs different? Are the submission and posting rules the same or different? How so?

1. Social media sites are run by librarians, generally in public service or communication roles.

2. Cooperative and collaborative. Librarians run social media, computing services runs the website. They have their rules, we have ours.

3. Front end development and social media positions are both in the reference services group.

4. I run the library's web site as the Systems Librarian. Because I oversee systems, of which the web site is a part, it is a part of my job description to provide technology troubleshooting and support to the rest of the library staff who utilize certain technologies, but who are not educated in the systems behind those technologies. Submission and posting rules follow our library's criteria for creating and posting online content.

5. We have an information literacy librarian taking the leadership on posting content to our various social media outlets. Library technology provides tech support.

6. We have a full-time Web Services Librarian who coordinates our website and presence in course management and campus portal; and leads a Library Web Improvement Team. We have a full-time communications manager (not a librarian) who coordinates all Marketing and Outreach for the department, including social media; and leads a Library Communication and Outreach Team. The Communications Manager is also member of the Web Team. The process for approving changes and new content posted to the website is separate from our social media process and policy. One difference between social media and web content processes is that anyone on staff can suggest web content; while not all staff are approved to post in social media channels.

7. Mostly run by the same person but occasionally another person helps out with the content scheduled for our social media sites.

8. I am the web coordinator. Someone on our Public Relations Committee manages our social media presence.

9. One person is responsible for the website. Others are responsible for Facebook, Twitter, and other social media sites. There is a concerted effort to be consistent across all venues, but no written policy at this time.

10. We don't participate in any social media sites.

11. The library's website currently constitutes our only online presence.

12. The library webmaster enforces consistency across social media platforms through regular review of the sites used. The sites are maintained by other librarians, primarily in Reference, as part of their duties due to the fact that our library only has the one person administering the website.

13. Social media is utilized by 3-4 librarians, including the one who manages the website. This is mostly on our WordPress blog which automatically updates our Facebook feed.

14. Social media sites are run by the university and the library website is run by the library IT. The staffs are different and the university social media has stricter submission and posting rules than the library.

15. Completely different. Content is submitted to those who control the site in order for it to be put up.

16. Web Designer (a member of the Library Information Technology unit) manages the library's website (design, technology, and posting of content created by others). Web Developer also manages the library's Twitter and Flickr accounts. Other library staff manage Facebook presence. Submissions to web pages subject to editorial review; postings to Facebook open to community.

17. More or less the same parties. More people are involved in social media than the website.

18. Two different people.

19. The library's website is managed by one librarian. The library's social media presence is managed primarily by the same librarian but also in coordination with one other librarian, two staff, and a handful of student workers. Since one person manages the entire primary website, it has no posting rules. Social media sites have a wide variety of rules, such as the type of content posted, guidelines for responding and liking posts, an editorial calendar, and image usage guidelines.

20. Same parties.

21. The Web Services Librarian (primary party responsible for the website) is also head of the Social Media Team. There is overlap between the Web Team (an advisory body) and the Social Media Team, but not 100%. Currently, only the Web Services Librarian and Head of Systems can add content directly to the website, aside from LibGuides. All members of the Social Media Team can add content to social media sites, and anyone in the library can suggest content. The best practices for social media are better-defined than the best practices for the website, because it is newer. (Best practices for the website are under development.)

22. They are administered by the same parties, although there are a few extra parties with permissions to post to social media sites (though they do not have permissions to edit website content).

23. Library social media is managed by different staff than of the website. They do work closely together and all serve on a committee that touches both areas.

24. The web development specialist participates in promoting library information on social media sites, but other staff and faculty from instruction and reference are also responsible for social media communications from/about the library.

25. All staff are able to added to the library's social media resources. Although, one librarian has the responsibility of updating the website or asking marketing to update the website.

26. Same.

27. Same person manages website and social media marketing efforts.

28. The library website and social media sites are run roughly by the same people. Both sites are used to disseminate practical information (hours changes, etc.) but on Facebook we also include more things like fun library stories, pictures, etc. That we do not post on the main library webpage. This allows us to communicate on a more informal level with students.

29. Collaboration between instructional librarian, web service librarian and other members of library stuff.

30. There is a team of staff who are working on developing a social media presence. The staff in charge of updating the website also sits on the social media team. Changes made to the website are less formalized than the rules around social media. The website is updated on an ad hoc basis, by one individual with expertise in writing for the web. The social media team, on the

other hand, must work together to ensure there are new postings on a regular basis, that the message is consistent across platforms, and that proper conventions are met.

31. The library website is managed by a standing web dev team, and the social media presence is generally managed by a marketing and communications team. The library communications director serves on both groups and helps coordinate content, stories, etc. across all platforms.

32. One person supervises the website and other librarians manage social media. The latter is more or less on hold due to lack of interest on the part of students.

33. Same parties.

34. The IT web staff assists the non technical employees in several aspects of the social media efforts. They work in conjunction, the submission and posting rules are the same.

35. The same person who is responsible for the library web site coordinates the library-related social media sites.

36. Same person (me). Do not have Facebook, YouTube, or Pinterest presence at moment. Minimal social media presence currently. Have a blog that feeds directly to Library website. Considering selective and strategic use of social media in future, if worth the time and effort involved.

37. Our college makes ALL updates to the library website, we only provide the content. Webpage management may change in the future if a CMS is installed. Different members of our library staff manage our various social media sites.

38. These are run by different people. The website is maintained by the Library Director, while one of the Library Specialists (one involved in Library events) handles the social media.

39. We do not have any social media sites.

40. The same parties.

41. Different staff check the website than the one who maintains the social media sites. Our website is overseen by college staff and we request changes that are permitted in accordance with our college "branding."

42. Different staff. We have a Web Services Librarian who designed, coded, and

maintains the library web site. We have an Outreach Services Librarian who manages our social media presence.

43. Same person.

44. Social media project started by the web services librarian, but those responsibilities are now given to a separate full-time reference librarian. So website and social media work together, but are managed by two different people.

45. Same librarian supervises social media - grants staff access for posting based on their technological experience and job capacity.

46. One technology librarian is both in charge of the website and co-runs our social media campaigns. He gets support from many other staff, primarily content editing. The staff who contribute to the website and social media do not overlap. The writing guidelines (which are largely ad hoc & unwritten) are very different for the website and social media. In particular, student workers contribute much social media content but do not have access to edit the website. Website content is primarily judged on its usability, concision, & clarity while social media content is meant to be more fun & free-spirited.

47. External social media library entities are ad hoc and run by interested staff and faculty. No formal relationship exists between Website Librarian (50% position started in 2012 from internal appointment) and external free library related entities. Website Librarian consults with "Web Advisory Group" voluntary working group who incidentally overlap with the individuals who run social media library entities.

48. Marketing runs this for the college.

49. Staff that run web site manage and coordinate social media accounts and integrate social media content into library home page, librarians populate social media accounts with content.

50. Our webmaster has access to all social media sites, however so do many of our librarians, so approximately five people contribute and maintain the social media presence. A librarian in technical services is considered the 'admin' on the social media pages (which is not the same department as the Systems Department, where the programmer sits).

51. We do not run any social media sites on the library website.

52. Different staff. Facebook and Twitter primarily used to promote library events

and news. News posted on the site. Pinterest and YouTube used for library instruction and collections promotion.

53. My library doesn't have too much to do with social media. We do participate in the college's Facebook posting and have a blog. I am the person who runs the library website and am in charge of posting information to the college's Facebook. The posts tend to be shorter versions of some of our blog entries. I run the blog more from the technical angle (WordPress updates, design, widget content) and our administrative assistant oversees the posts' content and the posting of our submissions.

54. The same person (me) manages the website and the social media for the library.

55. Staff are different, work independently, serve on the same website team. Both work with similar posting rules that adhere to campus wide guidelines

56. Library has no social media sites. We are hoping to add them when a new part-time employee is hired.

57. Same parties, but only one librarian heads up the social media outreach. We have additional staff who help with social media content creation, but they rotate. We wrote up separate guidelines for social media just to make sure we remain consistent.

Chapter 2: Content Editing

Table 2.1: Which phrase best describes your use of content editing or management systems for the library website?

	No Answer	Purchased a commercial system for the library	System provided by the college web staff	Adapted an open-source alternative	Program our own system
Entire sample	10.53%	10.53%	31.58%	24.56%	22.81%

Table 2.2: Which phrase best describes your use of content editing or management systems for the library website? Broken out by type of college.

Type of College	No Answer	Purchased a commercial system for the library	System provided by the college web staff	Adapted an open-source alternative	Program our own system
Community college	9.09%	22.73%	40.91%	18.18%	9.09%
4-year/MA-granting college	5.26%	5.26%	36.84%	21.05%	31.58%
PhD-granting college/Research university	18.75%	0.00%	12.50%	37.50%	31.25%

Table 2.3: Which phrase best describes your use of content editing or management systems for the library website? Broken out by public or private status of the college.

Public or Private	No Answer	Purchased a commercial system for the library	System provided by the college web staff	Adapted an open-source alternative	Program our own system
Public	11.90%	11.90%	28.57%	28.57%	19.05%
Private	6.67%	6.67%	40.00%	13.33%	33.33%

Table 2.4: Which phrase best describes your use of content editing or management systems for the library website? Broken out by full-time equivalent student enrollment of the college.

Enrollment	No Answer	Purchased a commercial system for the library	System provided by the college web staff	Adapted an open-source alternative	Program our own system
Less than 2,500	6.25%	25.00%	37.50%	12.50%	18.75%
2,500 to 7,499	0.00%	6.67%	33.33%	20.00%	40.00%
7,500 to 14,999	23.08%	7.69%	30.77%	15.38%	23.08%
15,000 or more	15.38%	0.00%	23.08%	53.85%	7.69%

Table 2.5: Does your library website use a content management system?

	No Answer	Yes	No
Entire sample	1.75%	64.91%	33.33%

Table 2.6: Does your library website use a content management system? Broken out by type of college.

Type of College	No Answer	Yes	No
Community college	4.55%	72.73%	22.73%
4-year/MA-granting college	0.00%	57.89%	42.11%
PhD-granting college/Research university	0.00%	62.50%	37.50%

Table 2.7: Does your library website use a content management system? Broken out by public or private status of the college.

Public or Private	No Answer	Yes	No
Public	2.38%	66.67%	30.95%
Private	0.00%	60.00%	40.00%

Table 2.8: Does your library website use a content management system? Broken out by full-time equivalent student enrollment of the college.

Enrollment	No Answer	Yes	No
Less than 2,500	0.00%	62.50%	37.50%
2,500 to 7,499	0.00%	66.67%	33.33%
7,500 to 14,999	0.00%	61.54%	38.46%
15,000 or more	7.69%	69.23%	23.08%

Table 2.9: If your library website does use a CMS, does it use the following?

Table 2.9A: Drupal

	Yes	No
Entire sample	32.43%	67.57%

Table 2.9B: e107

	Yes	No
Entire sample	0.00%	64.91%

Table 2.9C: Joomla

	Yes	No
Entire sample	2.70%	97.30%

Table 2.9D: Mambo

	Yes	No
Entire sample	2.70%	97.30%

Table 2.9E: ModX

	Yes	No
Entire sample	2.70%	97.30%

Table 2.9F: Plone

	Yes	No
Entire sample	2.70%	97.30%

Table 2.9G: TextPattern

	Yes	No
Entire sample	0.00%	100.00%

Table 2.9H: WordPress

	Yes	No
Entire sample	5.41%	94.59%

Table 2.9I: Zoop

	Yes	No
Entire sample	0.00%	100.00%

Table 2.10: If your library website does use a CMS, does it use the following? Broken out by type of college.

Table 2.10A: Drupal

Type of College	Yes	No
Community college	12.50%	87.50%
4-year/MA-granting college	45.45%	54.55%
PhD-granting college/Research university	50.00%	50.00%

Table 2.10B: Joomla

Type of College	Yes	No
Community college	6.25%	93.75%
4-year/MA-granting college	0.00%	100.00%
PhD-granting college/Research university	0.00%	100.00%

Table 2.10C: Mambo

Type of College	Yes	No
Community college	0.00%	100.00%
4-year/MA-granting college	0.00%	100.00%
PhD-granting college/Research university	10.00%	90.00%

Table 2.10D: ModX

Type of College	Yes	No
Community college	0.00%	100.00%
4-year/MA-granting college	9.09%	90.91%
PhD-granting college/Research university	0.00%	100.00%

Table 2.10E: Plone

Type of College	Yes	No
Community college	6.25%	93.75%
4-year/MA-granting college	0.00%	100.00%
PhD-granting college/Research university	0.00%	100.00%

Table 2.10F: WordPress

Type of College	Yes	No
Community college	0.00%	100.00%
4-year/MA-granting college	9.09%	90.91%
PhD-granting college/Research university	10.00%	90.00%

Table 2.11: If your library website does use a CMS, does it use the following? Broken out by public or private status of the college.

Table 2.11A: Drupal

Public or Private	Yes	No
Public	35.71%	64.29%
Private	22.22%	77.78%

Table 2.11B: Joomla

Public or Private	Yes	No
Public	3.57%	96.43%
Private	0.00%	100.00%

Table 2.11C: Mambo

Public or Private	Yes	No
Public	3.57%	96.43%
Private	0.00%	100.00%

Table 2.11D: ModX

Public or Private	Yes	No
Public	3.57%	96.43%
Private	0.00%	100.00%

Table 2.11E: Plone

Public or Private	Yes	No
Public	0.00%	100.00%
Private	11.11%	88.89%

Table 2.11F: WordPress

Public or Private	Yes	No
Public	3.57%	96.43%
Private	11.11%	88.89%

Table 2.12: If your library website does use a CMS, does it use the following? Broken out by full-time equivalent student enrollment of the college.

Table 2.12A: Drupal

Enrollment	Yes	No
Less than 2,500	20.00%	80.00%
2,500 to 7,499	30.00%	70.00%
7,500 to 14,999	25.00%	75.00%
15,000 or more	55.56%	44.44%

Table 2.12B: Joomla

Enrollment	Yes	No
Less than 2,500	0.00%	100.00%
2,500 to 7,499	10.00%	90.00%
7,500 to 14,999	0.00%	100.00%
15,000 or more	0.00%	100.00%

Table 2.12C: Mambo

Enrollment	Yes	No
Less than 2,500	0.00%	100.00%
2,500 to 7,499	0.00%	100.00%
7,500 to 14,999	0.00%	100.00%
15,000 or more	11.11%	88.89%

Table 2.12D: ModX

Enrollment	Yes	No
Less than 2,500	0.00%	100.00%
2,500 to 7,499	0.00%	100.00%
7,500 to 14,999	12.50%	87.50%
15,000 or more	0.00%	100.00%

Table 2.12E: Plone

Enrollment	Yes	No
Less than 2,500	10.00%	90.00%
2,500 to 7,499	0.00%	100.00%
7,500 to 14,999	0.00%	100.00%
15,000 or more	0.00%	100.00%

Table 2.12F: WordPress

Enrollment	Yes	No
Less than 2,500	0.00%	100.00%
2,500 to 7,499	10.00%	90.00%
7,500 to 14,999	0.00%	100.00%
15,000 or more	11.11%	88.89%

If the library uses a CMS not listed above, please specify.

1. Create production site with CS5, developed intranet on Drupal and to test for scalability/flexibility to run our main web site.

2. We are investigating Drupal but none is in place except we do use LibGuides but not for the full site.

3. We use LibGuides for a lot of things but our main page is provided by the college

4. dotCMS.

5. Marketing manages the library's website so I do not know.

6. Expression Web.

7. Typo3 supplemented by LibGuides, soon to convert to Drupal 7.

8. Sitecore.

9. Contribute.

10. Primo.

11. Adobe Contribute.

12. Ingeniux.

13. Reddot.

14. Ingeniux.

15. Google Sites.

16. Hannon Hill Cascade.

17. LibGuides.

Table 2.13: How satisfied are you with your existing content management system?

	No Answer	Quite satisfied	Satisfied	Not completely satisfied	We plan to change systems
Entire sample	14.04%	29.82%	31.58%	10.53%	14.04%

Table 2.14: How satisfied are you with your existing content management system? Broken out by type of college.

Type of College	No Answer	Quite satisfied	Satisfied	Not completely satisfied	We plan to change systems
Community college	9.09%	31.82%	36.36%	4.55%	18.18%
4-year/MA-granting college	15.79%	15.79%	42.11%	15.79%	10.53%
PhD-granting college/Research university	18.75%	43.75%	12.50%	12.50%	12.50%

Table 2.15: How satisfied are you with your existing content management system? Broken out by public or private status of the college.

Public or Private	No Answer	Quite satisfied	Satisfied	Not completely satisfied	We plan to change systems
Public	14.29%	30.95%	33.33%	9.52%	11.90%
Private	13.33%	26.67%	26.67%	13.33%	20.00%

Table 2.16: How satisfied are you with your existing content management system? Broken out by full-time equivalent student enrollment of the college.

Enrollment	No Answer	Quite satisfied	Satisfied	Not completely satisfied	We plan to change systems
Less than 2,500	18.75%	31.25%	31.25%	6.25%	12.50%
2,500 to 7,499	6.67%	26.67%	40.00%	6.67%	20.00%
7,500 to 14,999	23.08%	23.08%	38.46%	15.38%	0.00%
15,000 or more	7.69%	38.46%	15.38%	15.38%	23.08%

Table 2.17: In the last full semester, approximately how many library personnel entered content into the college library website?

	Mean	Median	Minimum	Maximum
Entire sample	7.97	3.00	0.00	100.00

Table 2.18: In the last full semester, approximately how many library personnel entered content into the college library website? Broken out by type of college.

Type of College	Mean	Median	Minimum	Maximum
Community college	2.20	1.00	0.00	15.00
4-year/MA-granting college	5.94	3.50	0.00	32.00
PhD-granting college/Research university	18.87	6.00	1.00	100.00

Table 2.19: In the last full semester, approximately how many library personnel entered content into the college library website? Broken out by public or private status of the college.

Public or Private	Mean	Median	Minimum	Maximum
Public	8.84	3.00	0.00	100.00
Private	5.67	2.00	0.00	40.00

Table 2.20: In the last full semester, approximately how many library personnel entered content into the college library website? Broken out by full-time equivalent student enrollment of the college.

Enrollment	Mean	Median	Minimum	Maximum
Less than 2,500	2.03	1.25	0.00	8.00
2,500 to 7,499	6.14	2.50	0.00	40.00
7,500 to 14,999	4.67	2.50	1.00	32.00
15,000 or more	20.31	10.00	1.00	100.00

Table 2.21: How satisfied are you with the consistency of style and brand presentation on your website?

	No Answer	Not an important goal	Not very satisfied	Somewhat satisfied	Generally satisfied
Entire sample	1.75%	1.75%	3.51%	19.30%	73.68%

Table 2.22: How satisfied are you with the consistency of style and brand presentation on your website? Broken out by type of college.

Type of College	No Answer	Not an important goal	Not very satisfied	Somewhat satisfied	Generally satisfied
Community college	0.00%	4.55%	9.09%	13.64%	72.73%
4-year/MA-granting college	5.26%	0.00%	0.00%	21.05%	73.68%
PhD-granting college/Research university	0.00%	0.00%	0.00%	25.00%	75.00%

Table 2.23: How satisfied are you with the consistency of style and brand presentation on your website? Broken out by public or private status of the college.

Public or Private	No Answer	Not an important goal	Not very satisfied	Somewhat satisfied	Generally satisfied
Public	0.00%	2.38%	4.76%	19.05%	73.81%
Private	6.67%	0.00%	0.00%	20.00%	73.33%

Table 2.24: How satisfied are you with the consistency of style and brand presentation on your website? Broken out by full-time equivalent student enrollment of the college.

Enrollment	No Answer	Not an important goal	Not very satisfied	Somewhat satisfied	Generally satisfied
Less than 2,500	6.25%	0.00%	12.50%	25.00%	56.25%
2,500 to 7,499	0.00%	0.00%	0.00%	20.00%	80.00%
7,500 to 14,999	0.00%	7.69%	0.00%	15.38%	76.92%
15,000 or more	0.00%	0.00%	0.00%	15.38%	84.62%

Table 2.25: How easy is it to use and manipulate the following types of information or perform the following operations in your content management system?

Table 2.25A: Position and manipulate videos

	No Answer	Very easy	Relatively easy	Possible but with some restraints	Possible but with many restraints	Not able to do
Entire sample	14.04%	14.04%	22.81%	22.81%	15.79%	10.53%

Table 2.25B: Enter the same content to multiple locations on the site at the same time

	No Answer	Very easy	Relatively easy	Possible but with some restraints	Possible but with many restraints	Not able to do
Entire sample	14.04%	19.30%	15.79%	15.79%	12.28%	22.81%

Table 2.25C: Easily enter charts, tables and other tabular data

	No Answer	Very easy	Relatively easy	Possible but with some restraints	Possible but with many restraints	Not able to do
Entire sample	12.28%	8.77%	22.81%	22.81%	19.30%	14.04%

Table 2.25D: Check the functionality of page links

	No Answer	Very easy	Relatively easy	Possible but with some restraints	Possible but with many restraints	Not able to do
Entire sample	12.28%	21.05%	31.58%	8.77%	17.54%	8.77%

Table 2.25E: Restrict a large number of content providers to be able to access only very specific areas on the site

	No Answer	Very easy	Relatively easy	Possible but with some restraints	Possible but with many restraints	Not able to do
Entire sample	17.54%	19.30%	10.53%	5.26%	24.56%	22.81%

Table 2.25F: Provide a report of content changes in a specified period of time

	No Answer	Very easy	Relatively easy	Possible but with some restraints	Possible but with many restraints	Not able to do
Entire sample	15.79%	12.28%	19.30%	3.51%	14.04%	35.09%

Table 2.26: How easy is it to use and manipulate the following types of information or perform the following operations in your content management system? Broken out by type of college.

Table 2.26A: Position and manipulate videos

Type of College	No Answer	Very easy	Relatively easy	Possible but with some restraints	Possible but with many restraints	Not able to do
Community college	9.09%	18.18%	13.64%	13.64%	22.73%	22.73%
4-year/MA-granting college	15.79%	15.79%	26.32%	31.58%	5.26%	5.26%
PhD-granting college/Research university	18.75%	6.25%	31.25%	25.00%	18.75%	0.00%

Table 2.26B: Enter the same content to multiple locations on the site at the same time

Type of College	No Answer	Very easy	Relatively easy	Possible but with some restraints	Possible but with many restraints	Not able to do
Community college	9.09%	9.09%	4.55%	27.27%	9.09%	40.91%
4-year/MA-granting college	15.79%	26.32%	21.05%	10.53%	15.79%	10.53%
PhD-granting college/Research university	18.75%	25.00%	25.00%	6.25%	12.50%	12.50%

Table 2.26C: Easily enter charts, tables and other tabular data

Type of College	No Answer	Very easy	Relatively easy	Possible but with some restraints	Possible but with many restraints	Not able to do
Community college	9.09%	0.00%	18.18%	22.73%	22.73%	27.27%
4-year/MA-granting college	15.79%	21.05%	21.05%	21.05%	15.79%	5.26%
PhD-granting college/Research university	12.50%	6.25%	31.25%	25.00%	18.75%	6.25%

Table 2.26D: Check the functionality of page links

Type of College	No Answer	Very easy	Relatively easy	Possible but with some restraints	Possible but with many restraints	Not able to do
Community college	9.09%	9.09%	40.91%	13.64%	27.27%	0.00%
4-year/MA-granting college	15.79%	21.05%	15.79%	10.53%	21.05%	15.79%
PhD-granting college/Research university	12.50%	37.50%	37.50%	0.00%	0.00%	12.50%

Table 2.26E: Restrict a large number of content providers to be able to access only very specific areas on the site

Type of College	No Answer	Very easy	Relatively easy	Possible but with some restraints	Possible but with many restraints	Not able to do
Community college	9.09%	18.18%	13.64%	4.55%	13.64%	40.91%
4-year/MA-granting college	26.32%	21.05%	5.26%	0.00%	36.84%	10.53%
PhD-granting college/Research university	18.75%	18.75%	12.50%	12.50%	25.00%	12.50%

Table 2.26F: Provide a report of content changes in a specified period of time

Type of College	No Answer	Very easy	Relatively easy	Possible but with some restraints	Possible but with many restraints	Not able to do
Community college	9.09%	4.55%	18.18%	9.09%	18.18%	40.91%
4-year/MA-granting college	21.05%	5.26%	21.05%	0.00%	15.79%	36.84%
PhD-granting college/Research university	18.75%	31.25%	18.75%	0.00%	6.25%	25.00%

Table 2.27: How easy is it to use and manipulate the following types of information or perform the following operations in your content management system? Broken out by public or private status of the college.

Table 2.27A: Position and manipulate videos

Public or Private	No Answer	Very easy	Relatively easy	Possible but with some restraints	Possible but with many restraints	Not able to do
Public	14.29%	14.29%	19.05%	26.19%	16.67%	9.52%
Private	13.33%	13.33%	33.33%	13.33%	13.33%	13.33%

Table 2.27B: Enter the same content to multiple locations on the site at the same time

Public or Private	No Answer	Very easy	Relatively easy	Possible but with some restraints	Possible but with many restraints	Not able to do
Public	16.67%	19.05%	19.05%	11.90%	9.52%	23.81%
Private	6.67%	20.00%	6.67%	26.67%	20.00%	20.00%

Table 2.27C: Easily enter charts, tables and other tabular data

Public or Private	No Answer	Very easy	Relatively easy	Possible but with some restraints	Possible but with many restraints	Not able to do
Public	14.29%	9.52%	19.05%	26.19%	16.67%	14.29%
Private	6.67%	6.67%	33.33%	13.33%	26.67%	13.33%

Table 2.27D: Check the functionality of page links

Public or Private	No Answer	Very easy	Relatively easy	Possible but with some restraints	Possible but with many restraints	Not able to do
Public	14.29%	23.81%	35.71%	7.14%	16.67%	2.38%
Private	6.67%	13.33%	20.00%	13.33%	20.00%	26.67%

Table 2.27E: Restrict a large number of content providers to be able to access only very specific areas on the site

Public or Private	No Answer	Very easy	Relatively easy	Possible but with some restraints	Possible but with many restraints	Not able to do
Public	14.29%	21.43%	11.90%	7.14%	23.81%	21.43%
Private	26.67%	13.33%	6.67%	0.00%	26.67%	26.67%

Table 2.28F: Provide a report of content changes in a specified period of time

Public or Private	No Answer	Very easy	Relatively easy	Possible but with some restraints	Possible but with many restraints	Not able to do
Public	16.67%	14.29%	21.43%	4.76%	11.90%	30.95%
Private	13.33%	6.67%	13.33%	0.00%	20.00%	46.67%

Table 2.29: How easy is it to use and manipulate the following types of information or perform the following operations in your content management system? Broken out by full-time equivalent student enrollment of the college.

Table 2.29A: Position and manipulate videos

Enrollment	No Answer	Very easy	Relatively easy	Possible but with some restraints	Possible but with many restraints	Not able to do
Less than 2,500	18.75%	12.50%	12.50%	18.75%	12.50%	25.00%
2,500 to 7,499	6.67%	26.67%	20.00%	20.00%	20.00%	6.67%
7,500 to 14,999	15.38%	7.69%	15.38%	38.46%	15.38%	7.69%
15,000 or more	15.38%	7.69%	46.15%	15.38%	15.38%	0.00%

Table 2.29B: Enter the same content to multiple locations on the site at the same time

Enrollment	No Answer	Very easy	Relatively easy	Possible but with some restraints	Possible but with many restraints	Not able to do
Less than 2,500	12.50%	12.50%	0.00%	25.00%	18.75%	31.25%
2,500 to 7,499	6.67%	20.00%	13.33%	20.00%	20.00%	20.00%
7,500 to 14,999	15.38%	23.08%	30.77%	15.38%	0.00%	15.38%
15,000 or more	23.08%	23.08%	23.08%	0.00%	7.69%	23.08%

Table 2.29C: Easily enter charts, tables and other tabular data

Enrollment	No Answer	Very easy	Relatively easy	Possible but with some restraints	Possible but with many restraints	Not able to do
Less than 2,500	12.50%	6.25%	25.00%	6.25%	25.00%	25.00%
2,500 to 7,499	6.67%	13.33%	13.33%	26.67%	26.67%	13.33%
7,500 to 14,999	15.38%	15.38%	23.08%	30.77%	7.69%	7.69%
15,000 or more	15.38%	0.00%	30.77%	30.77%	15.38%	7.69%

Table 2.29D: Check the functionality of page links

Enrollment	No Answer	Very easy	Relatively easy	Possible but with some restraints	Possible but with many restraints	Not able to do
Less than 2,500	12.50%	25.00%	31.25%	0.00%	25.00%	6.25%
2,500 to 7,499	6.67%	6.67%	26.67%	20.00%	20.00%	20.00%
7,500 to 14,999	15.38%	38.46%	30.77%	7.69%	7.69%	0.00%
15,000 or more	15.38%	15.38%	38.46%	7.69%	15.38%	7.69%

Table 2.29E: Restrict a large number of content providers to be able to access only very specific areas on the site

Enrollment	No Answer	Very easy	Relatively easy	Possible but with some restraints	Possible but with many restraints	Not able to do
Less than 2,500	25.00%	12.50%	6.25%	0.00%	31.25%	25.00%
2,500 to 7,499	13.33%	6.67%	13.33%	6.67%	20.00%	40.00%
7,500 to 14,999	15.38%	23.08%	15.38%	7.69%	23.08%	15.38%
15,000 or more	15.38%	38.46%	7.69%	7.69%	23.08%	7.69%

Table 2.29F: Provide a report of content changes in a specified period of time

Enrollment	No Answer	Very easy	Relatively easy	Possible but with some restraints	Possible but with many restraints	Not able to do
Less than 2,500	18.75%	0.00%	12.50%	6.25%	12.50%	50.00%
2,500 to 7,499	6.67%	6.67%	20.00%	0.00%	13.33%	53.33%
7,500 to 14,999	15.38%	23.08%	23.08%	0.00%	15.38%	23.08%
15,000 or more	23.08%	23.08%	23.08%	7.69%	15.38%	7.69%

Chapter 3: Programming

Table 3.1: What is the most commonly used scripting language employed by the library website?

	No Answer	Perl	JavaScript	CGI	PHP	Other
Entire sample	21.05%	5.26%	47.37%	1.75%	17.54%	7.02%

Table 3.2: What is the most commonly used scripting language employed by the library website? Broken out by type of college.

Type of College	No Answer	Perl	JavaScript	CGI	PHP	Other
Community college	36.36%	0.00%	59.09%	0.00%	0.00%	4.55%
4-year/MA-granting college	10.53%	0.00%	52.63%	0.00%	26.32%	10.53%
PhD-granting college/Research university	12.50%	18.75%	25.00%	6.25%	31.25%	6.25%

Table 3.3: What is the most commonly used scripting language employed by the library website? Broken out by public or private status of the college.

Public or Private	No Answer	Perl	JavaScript	CGI	PHP	Other
Public	21.43%	4.76%	45.24%	2.38%	19.05%	7.14%
Private	20.00%	6.67%	53.33%	0.00%	13.33%	6.67%

Table 3.4: What is the most commonly used scripting language employed by the library website? Broken out by full-time equivalent student enrollment of the college.

Enrollment	No Answer	Perl	JavaScript	CGI	PHP	Other
Less than 2,500	31.25%	0.00%	56.25%	0.00%	0.00%	12.50%
2,500 to 7,499	20.00%	6.67%	60.00%	0.00%	13.33%	0.00%
7,500 to 14,999	7.69%	0.00%	30.77%	7.69%	46.15%	7.69%
15,000 or more	23.08%	15.38%	38.46%	0.00%	15.38%	7.69%

If the library website uses a scripting language not listed above, please specify.

1. HTML.

2. Apache Velocity.

3. XML.

4. HTML5.

Table 3.5: What percentage of the total script work done in Perl, PHP, CGI, JavaScript, and other scripting languages for the library website in the past year was done by the following sources?

Table 3.5A: Library information technology personnel

	Mean	Median	Minimum	Maximum
Entire sample	30.00%	0.00%	0.00%	100.00%

Table 3.5B: MLS librarians

	Mean	Median	Minimum	Maximum
Entire sample	43.62%	7.50%	0.00%	100.00%

Table 3.5C: College administration information technology department

	Mean	Median	Minimum	Maximum
Entire sample	26.43%	0.00%	0.00%	100.00%

Table 3.5D: Outside consultant or freelancer

	Mean	Median	Minimum	Maximum
Entire sample	2.33%	0.00%	0.00%	80.00%

Table 3.6: What percentage of the total script work done in Perl, PHP, CGI, JavaScript, and other scripting languages for the library website in the past year was done by the following sources? Broken out by type of college.

Table 3.6A: Library information technology personnel

Type of College	Mean	Median	Minimum	Maximum
Community college	18.60%	0.00%	0.00%	100.00%
4-year/MA-granting college	15.17%	0.00%	0.00%	100.00%
PhD-granting college/Research university	53.27%	90.00%	0.00%	100.00%

Table 3.6B: MLS librarians

Type of College	Mean	Median	Minimum	Maximum
Community college	33.40%	0.00%	0.00%	100.00%
4-year/MA-granting college	65.00%	97.50%	0.00%	100.00%
PhD-granting college/Research university	36.73%	1.00%	0.00%	100.00%

Table 3.6C: College administration information technology department

Type of College	Mean	Median	Minimum	Maximum
Community college	47.67%	15.00%	0.00%	100.00%
4-year/MA-granting college	19.83%	0.00%	0.00%	95.00%
PhD-granting college/Research university	10.47%	0.00%	0.00%	100.00%

Table 3.6D: Outside consultant or freelancer

Type of College	Mean	Median	Minimum	Maximum
Community college	0.33%	0.00%	0.00%	5.00%
4-year/MA-granting college	0.00%	0.00%	0.00%	0.00%
PhD-granting college/Research university	6.20%	0.00%	0.00%	80.00%

Table 3.7: What percentage of the total script work done in Perl, PHP, CGI, JavaScript, and other scripting languages for the library website in the past year was done by the following sources? Broken out by public or private status of the college.

Table 3.7A: Library information technology personnel

Public or Private	Mean	Median	Minimum	Maximum
Public	32.58%	0.00%	0.00%	100.00%
Private	20.56%	0.00%	0.00%	95.00%

Table 3.7B: MLS librarians

Public or Private	Mean	Median	Minimum	Maximum
Public	42.33%	5.00%	0.00%	100.00%
Private	48.33%	30.00%	0.00%	100.00%

Table 3.7C: College administration information technology department

Public or Private	Mean	Median	Minimum	Maximum
Public	25.55%	0.00%	0.00%	100.00%
Private	29.67%	0.00%	0.00%	100.00%

Table 3.7D: Outside consultant or freelancer

Public or Private	Mean	Median	Minimum	Maximum
Public	2.58%	0.00%	0.00%	80.00%
Private	1.44%	0.00%	0.00%	10.00%

Table 3.8: What percentage of the total script work done in Perl, PHP, CGI, JavaScript, and other scripting languages for the library website in the past year was done by the following sources? Broken out by full-time equivalent student enrollment of the college.

Table 3.8A: Library information technology personnel

Enrollment	Mean	Median	Minimum	Maximum
Less than 2,500	21.89%	0.00%	0.00%	100.00%
2,500 to 7,499	8.18%	0.00%	0.00%	90.00%
7,500 to 14,999	26.00%	0.00%	0.00%	100.00%
15,000 or more	59.42%	87.50%	0.00%	100.00%

Table 3.8B: MLS librarians

Enrollment	Mean	Median	Minimum	Maximum
Less than 2,500	44.44%	5.00%	0.00%	100.00%
2,500 to 7,499	57.27%	100.00%	0.00%	100.00%
7,500 to 14,999	59.00%	75.00%	0.00%	100.00%
15,000 or more	17.67%	0.50%	0.00%	100.00%

Table 3.8C: College administration information technology department

Enrollment	Mean	Median	Minimum	Maximum
Less than 2,500	33.33%	2.00%	0.00%	100.00%
2,500 to 7,499	33.64%	0.00%	0.00%	100.00%
7,500 to 14,999	25.00%	0.00%	0.00%	100.00%
15,000 or more	15.83%	0.00%	0.00%	100.00%

Table 3.8D: Outside consultant or freelancer

Enrollment	Mean	Median	Minimum	Maximum
Less than 2,500	0.33%	0.00%	0.00%	3.00%
2,500 to 7,499	0.91%	0.00%	0.00%	10.00%
7,500 to 14,999	0.00%	0.00%	0.00%	0.00%
15,000 or more	7.08%	0.00%	0.00%	80.00%

Table 3.9: Does the library website use Cascading Style Sheets?

	Not at all	Moderately	Extensively	Not sure
Entire sample	7.02%	19.30%	64.91%	8.77%

Table 3.10: Does the library website use Cascading Style Sheets? Broken out by type of college.

Type of College	Not at all	Moderately	Extensively	Not sure
Community college	4.55%	31.82%	40.91%	22.73%
4-year/MA-granting college	10.53%	15.79%	73.68%	0.00%
PhD-granting college/Research university	6.25%	6.25%	87.50%	0.00%

Table 3.11: Does the library website use Cascading Style Sheets? Broken out by public or private status of the college.

Public or Private	Not at all	Moderately	Extensively	Not sure
Public	4.76%	21.43%	61.90%	11.90%
Private	13.33%	13.33%	73.33%	0.00%

Table 3.12: Does the library website use Cascading Style Sheets? Broken out by full-time equivalent student enrollment of the college.

Enrollment	Not at all	Moderately	Extensively	Not sure
Less than 2,500	6.25%	25.00%	43.75%	25.00%
2,500 to 7,499	20.00%	26.67%	53.33%	0.00%
7,500 to 14,999	0.00%	15.38%	76.92%	7.69%
15,000 or more	0.00%	7.69%	92.31%	0.00%

Table 3.13: Approximately what percentage of the library's Cascading Style Sheets are in the "embedded styles" format?

	Mean	Median	Minimum	Maximum
Entire sample	25.54%	10.00%	0.00%	100.00%

Table 3.14: Approximately what percentage of the library's Cascading Style Sheets are in the "embedded styles" format? Broken out by type of college.

Type of College	Mean	Median	Minimum	Maximum
Community college	7.28%	5.00%	0.50%	25.00%
4-year/MA-granting college	36.40%	10.00%	0.00%	100.00%
PhD-granting college/Research university	25.64%	10.00%	0.00%	100.00%

Table 3.15: Approximately what percentage of the library's Cascading Style Sheets are in the "embedded styles" format? Broken out by public or private status of the college.

Public or Private	Mean	Median	Minimum	Maximum
Public	23.81%	10.00%	0.00%	100.00%
Private	29.77%	10.00%	0.00%	100.00%

Table 3.16: Approximately what percentage of the library's Cascading Style Sheets are in the "embedded styles" format? Broken out by full-time equivalent student enrollment of the college.

Enrollment	Mean	Median	Minimum	Maximum
Less than 2,500	41.06%	25.00%	0.50%	100.00%
2,500 to 7,499	16.67%	10.00%	0.00%	100.00%
7,500 to 14,999	25.30%	7.50%	0.00%	100.00%
15,000 or more	21.73%	10.00%	0.00%	99.00%

Table 3.17: About what percentage of the routine content updates for the website are done through dynamic, database-driven web pages rather than through static pages?

	Mean	Median	Minimum	Maximum
Entire sample	31.26%	10.00%	0.00%	100.00%

Table 3.18: About what percentage of the routine content updates for the website are done through dynamic, database-driven web pages rather than through static pages? Broken out by type of college.

Type of College	Mean	Median	Minimum	Maximum
Community college	15.79%	0.50%	0.00%	100.00%
4-year/MA-granting college	27.82%	16.25%	0.00%	100.00%
PhD-granting college/Research university	47.81%	32.50%	0.00%	100.00%

Table 3.19: About what percentage of the routine content updates for the website are done through dynamic, database-driven web pages rather than through static pages? Broken out by public or private status of the college.

Public or Private	Mean	Median	Minimum	Maximum
Public	29.64%	10.00%	0.00%	100.00%
Private	35.58%	25.00%	0.00%	100.00%

Table 3.20: About what percentage of the routine content updates for the website are done through dynamic, database-driven web pages rather than through static pages? Broken out by full-time equivalent student enrollment of the college.

Enrollment	Mean	Median	Minimum	Maximum
Less than 2,500	29.00%	5.00%	0.00%	100.00%
2,500 to 7,499	24.20%	8.50%	0.00%	100.00%
7,500 to 14,999	20.63%	12.50%	0.00%	100.00%
15,000 or more	48.08%	25.00%	0.00%	100.00%

Table 3.21: Does the library website maintain an internal social bookmarking list or utilize an external bookmarking software or service (or else provide links to such a service)?

	No Answer	Internal social bookmarking lists	External bookmarking software or service	Links to bookmarking software or service
Entire sample	68.42%	5.26%	1.75%	24.56%

Table 3.22: Does the library website maintain an internal social bookmarking list or utilize an external bookmarking software or service (or else provide links to such a service)? Broken out by type of college.

Type of College	No Answer	Internal social bookmarking lists	External bookmarking software or service	Links to bookmarking software or service
Community college	81.82%	4.55%	0.00%	13.64%
4-year/MA-granting college	47.37%	5.26%	0.00%	47.37%
PhD-granting college/Research university	75.00%	6.25%	6.25%	12.50%

Table 3.23: Does the library website maintain an internal social bookmarking list or utilize an external bookmarking software or service (or else provide links to such a service)? Broken out by public or private status of the college.

Public or Private	No Answer	Internal social bookmarking lists	External bookmarking software or service	Links to bookmarking software or service
Public	64.29%	4.76%	0.00%	30.95%
Private	80.00%	6.67%	6.67%	6.67%

Table 3.24: Does the library website maintain an internal social bookmarking list or utilize an external bookmarking software or service (or else provide links to such a service)? Broken out by full-time equivalent student enrollment of the college.

Enrollment	No Answer	Internal social bookmarking lists	External bookmarking software or service	Links to bookmarking software or service
Less than 2,500	68.75%	6.25%	0.00%	25.00%
2,500 to 7,499	66.67%	6.67%	6.67%	20.00%
7,500 to 14,999	53.85%	7.69%	0.00%	38.46%
15,000 or more	84.62%	0.00%	0.00%	15.38%

Table 3.25: Does the library website offer mashups devised by library staff?

	No Answer	Yes	No
Entire sample	0.00%	12.28%	87.72%

Table 3.26: Does the library website offer mashups devised by library staff? Broken out by type of college.

Type of College	Yes	No
Community college	13.64%	86.36%
4-year/MA-granting college	10.53%	89.47%
PhD-granting college/Research university	12.50%	87.50%

Table 3.27: Does the library website offer mashups devised by library staff? Broken out by public or private status of the college.

Public or Private	Yes	No
Public	14.29%	85.71%
Private	6.67%	93.33%

Table 3.28: Does the library website offer mashups devised by library staff? Broken out by full-time equivalent student enrollment of the college.

Enrollment	Yes	No
Less than 2,500	12.50%	87.50%
2,500 to 7,499	13.33%	86.67%
7,500 to 14,999	7.69%	92.31%
15,000 or more	15.38%	84.62%

Table 3.29: Does the library website offer links to mashups devised by others?

	No Answer	Yes	No
Entire sample	0.00%	7.02%	92.98%

Table 3.30: Does the library website offer links to mashups devised by others? Broken out by type of college.

Type of College	Yes	No
Community college	4.55%	95.45%
4-year/MA-granting college	5.26%	94.74%
PhD-granting college/Research university	12.50%	87.50%

Table 3.31: Does the library website offer links to mashups devised by others? Broken out by public or private status of the college.

Public or Private	Yes	No
Public	9.52%	90.48%
Private	0.00%	100.00%

Table 3.32: Does the library website offer links to mashups devised by others? Broken out by full-time equivalent student enrollment of the college.

Enrollment	Yes	No
Less than 2,500	6.25%	93.75%
2,500 to 7,499	0.00%	100.00%
7,500 to 14,999	15.38%	84.62%
15,000 or more	7.69%	92.31%

Chapter 4: Federated Search

Table 4.1: How does your library handle federated search?

	No Answer	Uses a commercial discovery platform	Devised our own federated search engine	Does not emphasize federated search
Entire sample	1.75%	63.16%	1.75%	33.33%

Table 4.2: How does your library handle federated search? Broken out by type of college.

Type of College	No Answer	Uses a commercial discovery platform	Devised our own federated search engine	Does not emphasize federated search
Community college	0.00%	59.09%	0.00%	40.91%
4-year/MA-granting college	5.26%	63.16%	5.26%	26.32%
PhD-granting college/Research university	0.00%	68.75%	0.00%	31.25%

Table 4.3: How does your library handle federated search? Broken out by public or private status of the college.

Public or Private	No Answer	Uses a commercial discovery platform	Devised our own federated search engine	Does not emphasize federated search
Public	0.00%	66.67%	0.00%	33.33%
Private	6.67%	53.33%	6.67%	33.33%

Table 4.4: How does your library handle federated search? Broken out by full-time equivalent student enrollment of the college.

Enrollment	No Answer	Uses a commercial discovery platform	Devised our own federated search engine	Does not emphasize federated search
Less than 2,500	6.25%	56.25%	6.25%	31.25%
2,500 to 7,499	0.00%	46.67%	0.00%	53.33%
7,500 to 14,999	0.00%	84.62%	0.00%	15.38%
15,000 or more	0.00%	69.23%	0.00%	30.77%

Has your library altered the size, shape, graphic design, or placement of your website search boxes in recent years? If so, why? What have been the results?

1. We have left the search box largely alone for three years. Changes, like winter, are coming.

2. No.

3. No.

4. We place one search box above the fold.

5. Migrating to EDS and in doing so moved from a multi-tabbed metaphor and several search widgets to discrete parts of our collection to a single search box that serves as an API to EDS.

6. Yes, we've implemented searches on the main website just this semester. Students seem happy with the ease of use.

7. 2009 we made the search box more prominent on our homepage. We will be moving to a Discovery service soon (we currently have a federated search service but not discovery). It is used the most on our homepage.

8. Yes, when we went to a discovery service, we created a tabbed search box on our main page, so that patrons can choose what content they want to search.

9. We have placed a simple one on the front page of the website so that patrons can search the catalog quickly without having to click around. Feedback has been positive.

10. We have not.

11. The library website has undergone two iterations in the past three and a half years. During the first iteration, the website was streamlined so that related links appeared under a generic menu heading in an effort to help guide users to the resources they needed. The second iteration continued the menu/link relationship and included more data interaction with a MS SQL Server database as well as addressing accessibility issues.

12. Yes. We have moved our search box from the upper right hand corner of the page to our tabbed search on the homepage. Students were using the library search box to try and find articles and books. We found it best to remove this

search feature.

13. Boxes are larger and easier to use by people not use to searching.

14. We did. To give it more emphasis.

15. Yes - and in process of doing this once more. Has proven difficult because users believe they are searching the OPAC. In addition, mutliple OPACs - our own plus a consortial - have made our search box more difficult.

16. Our library had no website search boxes until 1.5 years ago, and adding them has dramatically increased the accessibility of our resources.

17. No.

18. Yes, we added a search box on the front page, in a prominent (but contextually unclear) place. It got used some. And then we moved it into a place where its context--searching for materials--was a little more clear, and use has skyrocketed.

19. Yes - we have made significant changes to the way we present search boxes on our website, with significant improvement in usability and user satisfaction (based on usage statistics and task-based usability testing).

20. The search boxes included throughout the website link to the catalog and to databases. There is a link to click to search the entire college website, including the library site. This model has not been altered recently.

21. Added more website search ability to the site with a site search box and with content filtering for research tools search. Removed Google search for university site to reduce confusion for patrons (they thought it was a catalog search).

22. No.

23. Yes - moved to a "tabbed search box" which allows the user to select which search tool they want to use.

24. We added a discovery service search box on the main library page in the summer of 2012.

25. Yes, to emphasize federated search.

26. Recently acquired a discovery layer and added the search box to the home

page. Recently added colour to make it stand out as students seemed to be overlooking it. Students seem to take more notice, now.

27. We were early adopters (2006) of a multi-tab system for selecting various discovery tools. We are working on a redesign now and are reducing the number of tabs. We have also placed site search in the header to separate it from catalog and metasearch boxes.

28. No.

29. Yes, there has been a prominent effort to place our discovery system up front on our website, and this will soon incorporate the website search site.

30. Yes. Excellent.

31. Added custom Google search box in 2009.

32. No.

33. We are using a smaller box to embed in LibGuides. This has allowed additional access, though we have not seen an enormous use of the smaller search box.

34. Yes, we added a catalog search box to homepage. We also updated on Millennium OPAC using OPAC refresher. It was dated. Looks great now. It is streamlined.

35. Smaller on every page.

36. We added a quick-search box to the homepage about a year ago. Response has been generally positive.

37. We've moved our search boxes on the library's homepage to the top left side of the page in 2010.

38. Library Web Site search box has maintained design. The "Quick Search" box has been more fully developed had been given more prominence on the front page. More students start their research at the quick box.

39. We're moving to a front-and-central tabbed search box which is obviously very common on library websites these days. Unfortunately, without a discovery layer (which we can't afford) we can't make some of the radical simplifications that I think would benefit students. I'd like to make the search box as large & prominent as possible.

40. Yes, moved to tabbed search offering catalog; e-book, e-journal list; home grown federated product; and commercial discovery service. still confusing, still unclear how it's being used. Have not performed user research on these questions.

41. Yes, each adjustment has improved use.

42. Very recently we have reduced the number of website search boxes on the main page. Specifically, we had tracked usage of the top box (we had 6 boxes before - 1 site search box, 1 FAQ, and 4 boxes on tabs) and replaced the top site search box with the FAQ based on statistical analysis of usage of that box. We're working to combine indexes from our FAQ with our Summon discovery service and site search so that over time, we only have ONE search box. We have noticed that most users just enter their search terms into the first box they see.

43. We added a search box for the federated search.

44. New website design launched last summer. Placed website search box in upper right for consistency with most web sites. User testing appears good.

45. Our search boxes used to be small and off to the side (took up about 1/4th to 1/5th of the page width). We've made it larger and placed it in the front and center (4/5th of page width). We've also reduced the clutter around the search box in order to make the search box itself more prominent. The decision was to make finding books and articles more noticeable and transformed the Library website from a mere informational tool to an online research tool. The new search box also looked more like the Google search format, which many people are familiar with. Students are more able to easily locate where to start their research.

46. In the past, we have used LibGuides, which has a static format, and now we are moving to Google Sites, which is still somewhat static, so we are constrained by their design of the search box.

47. We have content search boxes, but not search boxes that search the entire Library website.

48. Yes, the catalog search box is now no longer on the homepage-- big mistake! This will be changed soon when we redesign our website.

Describe what your library has done in the past three years to change its search interface to make it more attractive and effective for end users.

1. We have just started a redesign exploration.

2. Nothing. Ours is simple and we want to keep it that way.

3. We have started the process of our site redesign, which will focus on usability testing and website personas.

4. Less text; more "scannable" content; University site design under content management (Sharepoint), but the library was not included in the stakeholders who decided how the new site should be designed. As a result, as the library's webmaster, when the university web redesign was implemented, I insisted on receiving the files so I could create a static site that would look like the university's site in every way, though it is a static site, and I upgrade the code whenever the University templates change. I have since insisted on being considered a stakeholder in the University's web initiatives, and have been placed on the university's web committee.

5. Implemented an ERM module in our III catalog. Usability tests informed design and function. Created a tabbed search widget used on our homepage and in course management and campus portal allowing users to easily search for books, articles, and textbooks (course reserves).

6. We've implemented searches on the main website just this semester. Students seem happy with the ease of use.

7. Nothing on the homepage. We've done some tweaks to our Xerxes interface however.

8. We created a tabbed search box on our main page, so that patrons can choose what content they want to search, including discovery service, library catalog, journal articles (within discovery service) or journal/ebook titles.

9. We have not been able to change our interface because it is under the control of the campus webmaster.

10. In three years we have gone from a website that did not have a search interface to a homegrown search interface to having just purchased a commercial product to serve as the search interface. The commercial product is to be launched in January 2013.

11. We have updated our search fields into a tabbed field box.

12. Made more use of white space. Uses the "three click" format to reach information.

13. For catalog search, moved it from the middle of the page to the upper left. We have a search box for articles on the home page. Was able to finally convince people that we MUST have a general site search in the upper right hand corner.

14. We have done extensive usability testing with out users to refine our search box design, including better contextual help and clearer designation of search modes. We also changed the default search from title to keyword.

15. The website has been completely overhauled and rewritten from scratch, based on usability testing and card sorting.

16. We got a discovery service (instead of federated search) in the last three years. We have spent a lot of time trying to fix broken links within it.

17. Added a tabbed series of search boxes on the homepage to give quick access to popular search needs. Implemented a commercial discovery system with local branding. Recently modified the available search tabs, their labels, and their design/format based on usability testing (e.g., changed "Books & More" label to "Books & Ebooks" for catalog search; removed default description/instruction text from inside the search boxes to make them more visible AS search boxes; added specific radio button limiters to discovery system and catalog search boxes to simplify common search needs, etc.).

18. The library (and college) website search is now powered by Google. After making the change and local tweaking of the algorithms, search results are much more useful.

19. Redesigned for simplicity. Rebranded pages for consistency. Minimized style sheets, but increased control with style sheets. Added instant search with content filtering for finding research tools on the site (search results show as search is typed).

20. Made extensive use of LibGuides, paid close attention to accessibility and usability, implemented Serials Solutions SUMMON discovery tool, made website mobile-friendly.

21. We redesigned the main library homepage in 2012 to incorporate a single search box for our new discovery service.

22. Redesign phase1, currently in redesign phase 2 (usability study, plus testing).

23. See comment above about relocating site search. We do extensive user testing and adjust accordingly. In our forthcoming redesign, for example, we will be making article search more prominent, adding a dynamic daily hours section, and simplifying navigation on the homepage and site wide.

24. Small formatting changes within the limitations of the content management system.

25. A complete UI redesign and infrastructure development in 2012. An effort to perform usability studies and perform surveys was launched prior to and assisted in providing information to the developers and designers.

26. We redesigned our website to focus all search tools in the top quadrant of the site, in an interactive search interface and installed a discovery platform (we also federate - you seem to ask about federated and discovery systems in the same question, above). We also placed all high-level research support tools, such as citation generation tools, instant chat with a librarian, and direct links to course reserves, etc, in close proximity to the interactive research tools so that students would focus on the research process and the research tools that directly support that process. As a result our website is the highest used website in the college and students effectively access and take advantage of the increasing number of e-based resources.

27. Added Google search box. Redesigned home page and consistent navigation among all library pages using CSS. Cleaner layout; try to use common language (not library jargon).

28. Need to work on this.

29. Simplified the design to look a bit like Google and to remove unnecessary material.

30. Completed redid OPAC design and reviewed all functions using OPAC Refresher service from III.

31. Discovery.

32. Just subscribed to a discovery service.

33. We added a quick-search box to the homepage about a year ago. Response has been generally positive.

34. We've add mostly cosmetic changes - adding images and gradients, etc. We don't use federated searchings, so we have three search boxes on the library's homepage for the catalog, database links, and journal search.

35. Use of precise terminology -- but not "library language." Implemented LibGuides.

36. Box used to be in a neglected upper right-hand corner position, noticed by almost no one. We're putting it up front and giving users more choices. We went from just a catalog search to catalog, EBSCO databases, A to Z list, and LibGuides in a set of tabs.

37. Landing page: added a commercial discovery service option, added a home grown federated search option, peppered throughout site and LibGuides catalog search limited to e-books. Medical site pages: provided pubmed as default search.

38. Biannual usability studies resulting in rearranged and relabeled content.

39. We implemented Summon and reduced the number of search boxes on the front page. Currently we have two search boxes on the front page and we're trying to combine indexes to get that down to one.

40. Cleaned up the front page to be mostly direct search links and a few links to "other" library information.

41. Changed everything. Not really sure what you mean by "search interface" - how to search our site? Our resources?

42. We had a redesign of our entire website last year. The biggest change was the search box (described in the previous question). The search box had tabs for the different routes of researching (opac, databases, integrated search, eJournal finder, subject guides, website search). The integrated search used to be just an option in the databases option, but now has a tab and a search bar where users can just enter in search terms directly.

43. We have purchased CREDO, which is an e-reference subscription that also accesses other information resources. This makes it easier for students to find information.

Chapter 5: Website Marketing

Table 5.1: Does the library have a presence on any of the following social networking or file-sharing sites?

Table 5.1A: Twitter

	No Answer	Yes	No
Entire sample	0.00%	56.14%	43.86%

Table 5.1B: Pinterest

	No Answer	Yes	No
Entire sample	0.00%	24.56%	75.44%

Table 5.1C: YouTube

	No Answer	Yes	No
Entire sample	0.00%	50.88%	49.12%

Table 5.1D: Vimeo

	No Answer	Yes	No
Entire sample	0.00%	7.02%	92.98%

Table 5.1E: Facebook

	No Answer	Yes	No
Entire sample	0.00%	80.70%	19.30%

Table 5.2: Does the library have a presence on any of the following social networking or file-sharing sites? Broken out by type of college.

Table 5.2A: Twitter

Type of College	Yes	No
Community college	45.45%	54.55%
4-year/MA-granting college	57.89%	42.11%
PhD-granting college/Research university	68.75%	31.25%

Table 5.2B: Pinterest

Type of College	Yes	No
Community college	18.18%	81.82%
4-year/MA-granting college	31.58%	68.42%
PhD-granting college/Research university	25.00%	75.00%

Table 5.2C: YouTube

Type of College	Yes	No
Community college	45.45%	54.55%
4-year/MA-granting college	52.63%	47.37%
PhD-granting college/Research university	56.25%	43.75%

Table 5.2D: Vimeo

Type of College	Yes	No
Community college	0.00%	100.00%
4-year/MA-granting college	10.53%	89.47%
PhD-granting college/Research university	12.50%	87.50%

Table 5.2E: Facebook

Type of College	Yes	No
Community college	59.09%	40.91%
4-year/MA-granting college	94.74%	5.26%
PhD-granting college/Research university	93.75%	6.25%

Table 5.3: Does the library have a presence on any of the following social networking or file-sharing sites? Broken out by public or private status of the college.

Table 5.3A: Twitter

Public or Private	Yes	No
Public	61.90%	38.10%
Private	40.00%	60.00%

Table 5.3B: Pinterest

Public or Private	Yes	No
Public	23.81%	76.19%
Private	26.67%	73.33%

Table 5.3C: YouTube

Public or Private	Yes	No
Public	61.90%	38.10%
Private	20.00%	80.00%

Table 5.3D: Vimeo

Public or Private	Yes	No
Public	4.76%	95.24%
Private	13.33%	86.67%

Table 5.3E: Facebook

Public or Private	Yes	No
Public	78.57%	21.43%
Private	86.67%	13.33%

Table 5.4: Does the library have a presence on any of the following social networking or file-sharing sites? Broken out by full-time equivalent student enrollment of the college.

Table 5.4A: Twitter

Enrollment	Yes	No
Less than 2,500	43.75%	56.25%
2,500 to 7,499	40.00%	60.00%
7,500 to 14,999	46.15%	53.85%
15,000 or more	100.00%	0.00%

Table 5.4B: Pinterest

Enrollment	Yes	No
Less than 2,500	25.00%	75.00%
2,500 to 7,499	13.33%	86.67%
7,500 to 14,999	23.08%	76.92%
15,000 or more	38.46%	61.54%

Table 5.4C: YouTube

Enrollment	Yes	No
Less than 2,500	18.75%	81.25%
2,500 to 7,499	40.00%	60.00%
7,500 to 14,999	76.92%	23.08%
15,000 or more	76.92%	23.08%

Table 5.4D: Vimeo

Enrollment	Yes	No
Less than 2,500	12.50%	87.50%
2,500 to 7,499	0.00%	100.00%
7,500 to 14,999	7.69%	92.31%
15,000 or more	7.69%	92.31%

Table 5.4E: Facebook

Enrollment	Yes	No
Less than 2,500	68.75%	31.25%
2,500 to 7,499	73.33%	26.67%
7,500 to 14,999	84.62%	15.38%
15,000 or more	100.00%	0.00%

Table 5.5: Does the library maintain any blogs for the benefit of those patrons who want to keep up with library news?

	No Answer	Yes	No
Entire sample	0.00%	54.39%	45.61%

Table 5.6: Does the library maintain any blogs for the benefit of those patrons who want to keep up with library news? Broken out by type of college.

Type of College	Yes	No
Community college	45.45%	54.55%
4-year/MA-granting college	47.37%	52.63%
PhD-granting college/Research university	75.00%	25.00%

Table 5.7: Does the library maintain any blogs for the benefit of those patrons who want to keep up with library news? Broken out by public or private status of the college.

Public or Private	Yes	No
Public	59.52%	40.48%
Private	40.00%	60.00%

Table 5.8: Does the library maintain any blogs for the benefit of those patrons who want to keep up with library news? Broken out by full-time equivalent student enrollment of the college.

Enrollment	Yes	No
Less than 2,500	31.25%	68.75%
2,500 to 7,499	53.33%	46.67%
7,500 to 14,999	69.23%	30.77%
15,000 or more	69.23%	30.77%

Table 5.9: Does the library maintain any listservs for the benefit of those patrons who want to keep up with library news?

	No Answer	Yes	No
Entire sample	0.00%	7.02%	92.98%

Table 5.10: Does the library maintain any listservs for the benefit of those patrons who want to keep up with library news? Broken out by type of college.

Type of College	Yes	No
Community college	0.00%	100.00%
4-year/MA-granting college	5.26%	94.74%
PhD-granting college/Research university	18.75%	81.25%

Table 5.11: Does the library maintain any listservs for the benefit of those patrons who want to keep up with library news? Broken out by public or private status of the college.

Public or Private	Yes	No
Public	4.76%	95.24%
Private	13.33%	86.67%

Table 5.12: Does the library maintain any listservs for the benefit of those patrons who want to keep up with library news? Broken out by full-time equivalent student enrollment of the college.

Enrollment	Yes	No
Less than 2,500	0.00%	100.00%
2,500 to 7,499	13.33%	86.67%
7,500 to 14,999	0.00%	100.00%
15,000 or more	15.38%	84.62%

Table 5.13: Does the library maintain any RSS feeds for the benefit of those patrons who want to keep up with library news?

	No Answer	Yes	No
Entire sample	0.00%	42.11%	57.89%

Table 5.14: Does the library maintain any RSS feeds for the benefit of those patrons who want to keep up with library news? Broken out by type of college.

Type of College	Yes	No
Community college	27.27%	72.73%
4-year/MA-granting college	36.84%	63.16%
PhD-granting college/Research university	68.75%	31.25%

Table 5.15: Does the library maintain any RSS feeds for the benefit of those patrons who want to keep up with library news? Broken out by public or private status of the college.

Public or Private	Yes	No
Public	52.38%	47.62%
Private	13.33%	86.67%

Table 5.16: Does the library maintain any RSS feeds for the benefit of those patrons who want to keep up with library news? Broken out by full-time equivalent student enrollment of the college.

Enrollment	Yes	No
Less than 2,500	18.75%	81.25%
2,500 to 7,499	33.33%	66.67%
7,500 to 14,999	46.15%	53.85%
15,000 or more	76.92%	23.08%

Table 5.17: Does the library produce any podcasts for the benefit of those patrons who want to keep up with library news?

	No Answer	Yes	No
Entire sample	0.00%	1.75%	98.25%

Table 5.18: Does the library produce any podcasts for the benefit of those patrons who want to keep up with library news? Broken out by type of college.

Type of College	Yes	No
Community college	0.00%	100.00%
4-year/MA-granting college	0.00%	100.00%
PhD-granting college/Research university	6.25%	93.75%

Table 5.19: Does the library produce any podcasts for the benefit of those patrons who want to keep up with library news? Broken out by public or private status of the college.

Public or Private	Yes	No
Public	2.38%	97.62%
Private	0.00%	100.00%

Table 5.20: Does the library produce any podcasts for the benefit of those patrons who want to keep up with library news? Broken out by full-time equivalent student enrollment of the college.

Enrollment	Yes	No
Less than 2,500	0.00%	100.00%
2,500 to 7,499	0.00%	100.00%
7,500 to 14,999	0.00%	100.00%
15,000 or more	7.69%	92.31%

Table 5.21: Does the library send out any email newsletters for the benefit of those patrons who want to keep up with library news?

	No Answer	Yes	No
Entire sample	0.00%	31.58%	68.42%

Table 5.22: Does the library send out any email newsletters for the benefit of those patrons who want to keep up with library news? Broken out by type of college.

Type of College	Yes	No
Community college	9.09%	90.91%
4-year/MA-granting college	26.32%	73.68%
PhD-granting college/Research university	68.75%	31.25%

Table 5.23: Does the library send out any email newsletters for the benefit of those patrons who want to keep up with library news? Broken out by public or private status of the college.

Public or Private	Yes	No
Public	28.57%	71.43%
Private	40.00%	60.00%

Table 5.24: Does the library send out any email newsletters for the benefit of those patrons who want to keep up with library news? Broken out by full-time equivalent student enrollment of the college.

Enrollment	Yes	No
Less than 2,500	12.50%	87.50%
2,500 to 7,499	33.33%	66.67%
7,500 to 14,999	30.77%	69.23%
15,000 or more	53.85%	46.15%

Table 5.25: How many separate RSS feeds or electronic newsletters about the library and its services can be subscribed to from the library website?

	Mean	Median	Minimum	Maximum
Entire sample	6.00	1.00	0.00	126.00

Table 5.26: How many separate RSS feeds or electronic newsletters about the library and its services can be subscribed to from the library website? Broken out by type of college.

Type of College	Mean	Median	Minimum	Maximum
Community college	9.50	1.00	0.00	126.00
4-year/MA-granting college	1.43	1.00	0.00	10.00
PhD-granting college/Research university	6.08	1.00	0.00	40.00

Table 5.27: How many separate RSS feeds or electronic newsletters about the library and its services can be subscribed to from the library website? Broken out by public or private status of the college.

Public or Private	Mean	Median	Minimum	Maximum
Public	7.67	1.00	0.00	126.00
Private	1.42	0.00	0.00	10.00

Table 5.28: How many separate RSS feeds or electronic newsletters about the library and its services can be subscribed to from the library website? Broken out by full-time equivalent student enrollment of the college.

Enrollment	Mean	Median	Minimum	Maximum
Less than 2,500	0.38	0.00	0.00	1.00
2,500 to 7,499	1.67	1.00	0.00	10.00
7,500 to 14,999	5.44	1.00	0.00	35.00
15,000 or more	17.82	2.00	0.00	126.00

Table 5.29: What is the total number of subscribers to the electronic newsletters and RSS feeds offered by the library?

	Mean	Median	Minimum	Maximum
Entire sample	29.17	0.00	0.00	500.00

Table 5.30: What is the total number of subscribers to the electronic newsletters and RSS feeds offered by the library? Broken out by type of college.

Type of College	Mean	Median	Minimum	Maximum
Community college	16.60	0.00	0.00	150.00
4-year/MA-granting college	74.71	0.00	0.00	500.00
PhD-granting college/Research university	1.57	0.00	0.00	9.00

Table 5.31: What is the total number of subscribers to the electronic newsletters and RSS feeds offered by the library? Broken out by public or private status of the college.

Public or Private	Mean	Median	Minimum	Maximum
Public	43.56	0.50	0.00	500.00
Private	0.38	0.00	0.00	2.00

Table 5.32: What is the total number of subscribers to the electronic newsletters and RSS feeds offered by the library? Broken out by full-time equivalent student enrollment of the college.

Enrollment	Mean	Median	Minimum	Maximum
Less than 2,500	1.25	0.00	0.00	10.00
2,500 to 7,499	84.17	0.50	0.00	500.00
7,500 to 14,999	7.25	4.50	0.00	20.00
15,000 or more	26.00	1.50	0.00	150.00

Table 5.33: Does your website include personal customization features that enable end users to construct their own personal "my Library" identity, enabling them to save research strategies, favorite places, and/or other commonly used library resources?

	Yes	No	No, but we are planning on it
Entire sample	19.30%	73.68%	7.02%

Table 5.34: Does your website include personal customization features that enable end users to construct their own personal "my Library" identity, enabling them to save research strategies, favorite places, and/or other commonly used library resources? Broken out by type of college.

Type of College	Yes	No	No, but we are planning on it
Community college	27.27%	68.18%	4.55%
4-year/MA-granting college	15.79%	73.68%	10.53%
PhD-granting college/Research university	12.50%	81.25%	6.25%

Table 5.35: Does your website include personal customization features that enable end users to construct their own personal "my Library" identity, enabling them to save research strategies, favorite places, and/or other commonly used library resources? Broken out by public or private status of the college.

Public or Private	Yes	No	No, but we are planning on it
Public	26.19%	69.05%	4.76%
Private	0.00%	86.67%	13.33%

Table 5.36: Does your website include personal customization features that enable end users to construct their own personal "my Library" identity, enabling them to save research strategies, favorite places, and/or other commonly used library resources? Broken out by full-time equivalent student enrollment of the college.

Enrollment	Yes	No	No, but we are planning on it
Less than 2,500	18.75%	68.75%	12.50%
2,500 to 7,499	20.00%	73.33%	6.67%
7,500 to 14,999	23.08%	76.92%	0.00%
15,000 or more	15.38%	76.92%	7.69%

Describe what steps the library has taken, if any, to customize or personalize the library website.

1. We launched a "library favorites" tool that allows users to save catalog items, articles from Summon, journals, and databases to their account and organize them into folders.

2. None.

3. None as yet.

4. We've added a "glamor strip" to the top of our web index page (launching 1/13) that features pics and stories about faculty and staff who share their experiences using our library.

5. We cannot do this until the college moves to a CMS - hopefully in the next year. We have spent more time discussing ways to offer customization within our course management system.

6. None. We do offer some personalization within Xerxes in terms of saving records.

7. None, only available within the ILS, discovery service, and database vendor interfaces.

8. Users can log into an account to view lists of materials and renew checked out items.

9. Through the university Jnet site users can customize how they search and the type of information they receive.

10. We created "launching pages" for 3 demographics - faculty, graduate students and undergrads.

11. LibGuides.

12. None.

13. We would love to implement a "my Library" solution to allow personalization of the library website. Unfortunately we are unsure exactly how to begin and, having only one full-time person working on the site, really don't have the capability right now. So there are currently no "personalization" options on our site.

14. Users can create lists of materials in our catalog, view holds, checked out content and due dates.

15. None.

16. None.

17. The individual databases that the library subscribes to for the university offer personalized "save my searches" functionality. Customization is by subject, not by user roles.

18. Not as yet. But we will be going through a website redesign, and I think this may be something that we will look into.

19. We are developing a set of personally configurable WordPress plugins for students, faculty, and groups to add to their sites. (We have a campus wide WordPress services.)

20. None.

21. Customization is available only through partner vendor products. Students are encouraged, and heavily use customization features to create their own accounts for storing research and for creating and storing bibliographic research in citation management tools.

22. We rotate images and slideshows of images on a regular basis (approximately every two weeks) with many of the images coming from current library displays or library events marketing.

23. Only what is available in the OPAC.

24. Not much. We share access to the discovery tool among other schools and have chosen the barebones look. Only our logo and a link back to our webpage are different.

25. None.

26. None, really. All user traffic is anonymous (Drupal speak for not-signed-in) and we haven't tried to create accounts for students that would provide custom functionality.

27. Currently, users can track their search results and their library account, however we have considered implementing pages that specifically address their coursework, etc. by integrating their accounts with our student

management systems.

28. The Library website redesign we had last year deviated from the cluttered look of the College website.

29. Purchased LibGuides and created LibGuide subject guides for different deparments, adding more all the time.

30. None.

Table 5.37: On average, approximately how many hours per month does the library spend working on search engine optimization for the library website?

	Mean	Median	Minimum	Maximum
Entire sample	8.61	0.00	0.00	140.00

Table 5.38: On average, approximately how many hours per month does the library spend working on search engine optimization for the library website? Broken out by type of college.

Type of College	Mean	Median	Minimum	Maximum
Community college	2.18	0.00	0.00	25.00
4-year/MA-granting college	5.67	0.00	0.00	60.00
PhD-granting college/Research university	18.83	2.00	0.00	140.00

Table 5.39: On average, approximately how many hours per month does the library spend working on search engine optimization for the library website? Broken out by public or private status of the college.

Public or Private	Mean	Median	Minimum	Maximum
Public	5.85	0.00	0.00	140.00
Private	18.80	0.50	0.00	100.00

Table 5.40: On average, approximately how many hours per month does the library spend working on search engine optimization for the library website? Broken out by full-time equivalent student enrollment of the college.

Enrollment	Mean	Median	Minimum	Maximum
Less than 2,500	1.00	0.00	0.00	5.00
2,500 to 7,499	23.54	0.00	0.00	140.00
7,500 to 14,999	1.23	0.00	0.00	5.00
15,000 or more	6.17	4.00	0.00	25.00

Table 5.41: Approximately how many hours per month does the library spend in updating its presence on Facebook, Twitter, YouTube, Pinterest, Vimeo, and other such social media sites?

	Mean	Median	Minimum	Maximum
Entire sample	12.04	7.00	0.00	100.00

Table 5.42: Approximately how many hours per month does the library spend in updating its presence on Facebook, Twitter, YouTube, Pinterest, Vimeo, and other such social media sites? Broken out by type of college.

Type of College	Mean	Median	Minimum	Maximum
Community college	10.06	5.00	0.00	50.00
4-year/MA-granting college	13.59	8.00	3.00	100.00
PhD-granting college/Research university	12.67	10.00	0.00	40.00

Table 5.43: Approximately how many hours per month does the library spend in updating its presence on Facebook, Twitter, YouTube, Pinterest, Vimeo, and other such social media sites? Broken out by public or private status of the college.

Public or Private	Mean	Median	Minimum	Maximum
Public	11.43	5.00	0.00	100.00
Private	13.77	10.00	0.00	50.00

Table 5.44: Approximately how many hours per month does the library spend in updating its presence on Facebook, Twitter, YouTube, Pinterest, Vimeo, and other such social media sites? Broken out by full-time equivalent student enrollment of the college.

Enrollment	Mean	Median	Minimum	Maximum
Less than 2,500	17.54	7.00	0.00	100.00
2,500 to 7,499	5.62	5.00	0.00	10.00
7,500 to 14,999	7.54	5.00	0.00	30.00
15,000 or more	17.54	12.50	3.00	50.00

Chapter 6: Redesign

Table 6.1: Within the past year, has the library launched any kind of major website redesign?

	No Answer	Yes	No
Entire sample	1.75%	43.86%	54.39%

Table 6.2: Within the past year, has the library launched any kind of major website redesign? Broken out by type of college.

Type of College	No Answer	Yes	No
Community college	4.55%	36.36%	59.09%
4-year/MA-granting college	0.00%	36.84%	63.16%
PhD-granting college/Research university	0.00%	62.50%	37.50%

Table 6.3: Within the past year, has the library launched any kind of major website redesign? Broken out by public or private status of the college.

Public or Private	No Answer	Yes	No
Public	0.00%	47.62%	52.38%
Private	6.67%	33.33%	60.00%

Table 6.4: Within the past year, has the library launched any kind of major website redesign? Broken out by full-time equivalent student enrollment of the college.

Enrollment	No Answer	Yes	No
Less than 2,500	6.25%	31.25%	62.50%
2,500 to 7,499	0.00%	46.67%	53.33%
7,500 to 14,999	0.00%	38.46%	61.54%
15,000 or more	0.00%	61.54%	38.46%

Table 6.5: Does the library plan any major redesign of the library website within the next two years?

	No Answer	Yes	No
Entire sample	3.51%	56.14%	40.35%

Table 6.6: Does the library plan any major redesign of the library website within the next two years? Broken out by type of college.

Type of College	No Answer	Yes	No
Community college	9.09%	45.45%	45.45%
4-year/MA-granting college	0.00%	57.89%	42.11%
PhD-granting college/Research university	0.00%	68.75%	31.25%

Table 6.7: Does the library plan any major redesign of the library website within the next two years? Broken out by public or private status of the college.

Public or Private	No Answer	Yes	No
Public	2.38%	57.14%	40.48%
Private	6.67%	53.33%	40.00%

Table 6.8: Does the library plan any major redesign of the library website within the next two years? Broken out by full-time equivalent student enrollment of the college.

Enrollment	No Answer	Yes	No
Less than 2,500	12.50%	37.50%	50.00%
2,500 to 7,499	0.00%	53.33%	46.67%
7,500 to 14,999	0.00%	53.85%	46.15%
15,000 or more	0.00%	84.62%	15.38%

If the library is planning a redesign within the next two years, what do you think that the major goals of this redesign might be?

1. User experience accessibility.

2. Implement a content management system. Simplify the design. Have a student-driven design.

3. The redesign should reflect the move toward mobile computing; less text, easier navigation.

4. Better directory structure, eliminating all unnecessary or moribund files, integration of discovery layer, better use of space for "how do I?" and "what's new?", and a more personalized approach that displays success stories students/faculty/staff have had using our library.

5. Further simplification of content, implementation of CMS to improve maintenance and quality control; and to involve more staff in content creation and maintenance.

6. Improving and updating look. Incorporating discovery search interface.

7. To update and bring the library website more in line with the school's website.

8. Simplification.

9. The major goals of the redesign will be to add more information to the site and to make it more user friendly.

10. Usability, mobile integration, updated graphics.

11. Make the site responsive; implement a content management system; improve usability.

12. Integrating several unit-specific and unit-managed sites (all different in design) into the larger site for consistency or presentation and navigation.

13. A more streamlined search interface, hopefully based on a discovery service such as Summon.

14. Consistency with university-wide site redesign that is underway. Streamlining of main menu options to de-clutter the homepage (more emphasis on expanding submenus). Enhanced visual appeal. More visibility of social media

sites.

15. Better mobile experience, higher accessibility level, integration with upcoming new ILS.

16. Library will be using the college's template to create a new website.

17. Primarily to implement or improve current functionality within the Drupal 7 framework.

18. We are hoping that the university will acquire a content management system.

19. Responsive web design page plus user-friendlier site.

20. Improved Library branding. Better navigation.

21. Improved usability and discoverability of content, more dynamic (dbase-driven) content, and a more compelling graphical presence for features.

22. To incorporate responsive design into the site as an alternative to maintaining the pared down mobile secondary site.

23. Cleaner interface; federated search (if we can get a new LMS/OPAC); more social media.

24. Our college plans to implement a new CMS within the next year.

25. 1) To own our own website (currently the majority of the "look" of the site is locked by a 3rd party vendor due to contract), 2) Make the site more uniform and easy to use, and 3) Include more dynamic content

26. Customization for each person; more interactive.

27. The major goals are to reduce the number of clicks to 90% of the library's online resources from 4 to 2. Additionally, the secondary goal is to reduce the content on the library's homepage.

28. Re-evaluate opportunities offered by new LMS. Integrate customization options.

29. New CMS. More flexible templates. An ideal new design would account for a widely different number of devices and screen sizes/resolutions accessing it.

30. Improved usability, incorporating new content/technologies, branding and

aesthetic improvements.

31. Reducing the noise on the front page and designing for discovery based on results of usability testing.

32. To simplify the website greatly and to make it mobile friendly.

If the library has done a redesign within the past two years, what did this redesign accomplish?

1. Consistency of design; easier to identify a research starting point.

2. Better functionality, better integration and consistency of interior pages, better and more consistent navigation.

3. Incorporated feedback from usability tests to offer easier access to the most needed content, focus and review of existing content.

4. Ease of use, streamlined content, usability testing, a lot less text.

5. Removing bad links and obsolete pages.

6. We have improved the usability of our online databases page.

7. Our most recent redesign incorporated more interactivity with our back-end database as well as addressing accessibility issues, specifically Section 508 and WCAG 3.

8. Cleaner format, easier to search and read.

9. Changed presentation from library-centric (with heavy use of library jargon and department presence) to user-centric (with emphasis on services and material type rather than library departments).

10. Created a more intuitive organization scheme. Created visual continuity with the university's primary website. Implemented API mashups and other dynamic AJAX content. Created a new library brand logo. Incorporated a social media presence. Added Google Analytics to track usage.

11. Moved the library from a static website to a CMS. Added search limiters, built in statistical capabilities, made content administration easier.

12. Streamlined look and feel to entire site. Consistency across all pages. Better navigation.

13. We redesigned the main library page to make it more user friendly and incorporate a search box for discovery.

14. Modern design.

15. In process, has not yet launched. Yet, we are pretty confident that we did well in not only restructuring the site but in evaluating all aspects of the content.

16. Cleaner, more modern home page; better organized; more flexibility for dynamic content; push technology for library news.

17. OPAC is easier to use. All colleges within the district have same functionality. Modern headers. Turned on new OPAC features. Website is easier to use, more organized.

18. Consistent, usable navigation via a rigorously tested user-centered usability study of our information architecture.

19. The last redesign in 2010 was solely to update some dynamic features, add new components like a chat widget, and to add more graphics to a heavily text based site.

20. Cleaner interface. Moved to college CMS.

21. We moved to a CMS from static files. We instituted some basic standards, like human-readable URLs, plain language, Google analytics on every page, reordering links based on usage, trimming difficult to maintain or underused content. Site has more dynamic features now. Editing web content is much easier for library staff as well.

22. Improved usability, incorporated new technologies, branding and aesthetic improvements.

23. We adopted the new template of the university (which is changing now again) and tried to incorporate social media and event driven elements.

24. Standardization across site and within University graphical guidelines; improved wayfinding on site; commercial discovery service implemented; significant improvement in time and ability of content authors to update and improve content easily.

25. The redesign allowed for an easier to navigate and uncluttered interface for the users. Many of the responses to the redesign has been how great it looks and how the new website has been so much easier to use.

26. We are in the process of improving the usability and design of our website.

27. Made it easier to update web pages, easier for students to find information, and for information resources to be used.

What is the single best product or idea that you have discovered in recent years that has most helped you to improve the library website?

1. Drupal.

2. A CMS that will allow the administrator to restrict access based on group or content area.

3. Google analytics.

4. Adobe CS5.

5. Drupal.

6. Asking for library faculty to be given access to the website for editing purposes was a great idea.

7. I use website apps in Google Chrome to analyze the pre- and post-processed PHP content for troubleshooting.

8. Consistent usability testing.

9. QR codes on the LibGuides so students can access on iPad, iPhone, etc.

10. Usability testing - a consistent, regular program of bi-monthly usability tests on a variety of library pages.

11. LibGuides.

12. Integrating search boxes directly into the page.

13. Summon.

14. SiteImprove - The campus IT department subscribed to this product and gave the library webmaster access. This has helped us to significantly clean up spelling in our content and correct broken links. We are also just now starting to use it to correct HTML and CSS validation errors and improve accessibility, and we are excited about the improvements that will bring.

15. The CMS itself, Drupal.

16. JavaScript and AJAX.

17. LibGuides - including their mobile site builder add-on. It's made a HUGE

difference in how easy it is for us to create research guides and course-specific guides. It's incredibly easy to integrate library content into the university course management system, too.

18. Single search box.

19. Adopting content management -- Sitellite (2006-2012); Drupal (2012-present).

20. Drupal.

21. jquery.

22. Blogger--use to update library news information--allows for remote updating/push to website with RSS through Feedburner. Increased use of CSS has helped--want to explore/enhance further.

23. Less is more.

24. Stable URLs to database material.

25. LibraryH3lp chat service.

26. Usability Testing!

27. Google Analytics - we know how the site is being used, shows us where to improve, and has helped us reduce 404 errors

28. understanding CMS

29. DRUPAL DRUPAL DRUPAL DRUPAL DRUPAL DRUPAL DRUPAL DRUPAL DRUPAL DRUPAL DRUPAL DRUPAL DRUPAL DRUPAL DRUPAL.

30. LibGuides.

31. libraryh3lp.com.

32. Summon has been a great first step to reducing the number of search boxes. I don't think our students really understand the different purposes of the different search boxes (they just enter search terms), so being able to reduce the boxes is very important to us.

33. SiteImprove.com to track broken links and misspellings.

34. Google products and inter-functionality.

35. LibGuides.

36. Mobile friendly versions/coding/CMSs.

Chapter 7: Library Website Budget

Table 7.1: Is the budget for the library website a separate line item in the library's budget or is it considered part of the library's IT budget?

	No Answer	Separate line item in the library budget	Part of the library IT budget	Part of the college IT budget
Entire sample	8.77%	1.75%	56.14%	33.33%

Table 7.2: Is the budget for the library website a separate line item in the library's budget or is it considered part of the library's IT budget? Broken out by type of college.

Type of College	No Answer	Separate line item in the library budget	Part of the library IT budget	Part of the college IT budget
Community college	4.55%	0.00%	45.45%	50.00%
4-year/MA-granting college	15.79%	0.00%	57.89%	26.32%
PhD-granting college/Research university	6.25%	6.25%	68.75%	18.75%

Table 7.3: Is the budget for the library website a separate line item in the library's budget or is it considered part of the library's IT budget? Broken out by public or private status of the college.

Public or Private	No Answer	Separate line item in the library budget	Part of the library IT budget	Part of the college IT budget
Public	0.00%	2.38%	64.29%	33.33%
Private	33.33%	0.00%	33.33%	33.33%

Table 7.4: Is the budget for the library website a separate line item in the library's budget or is it considered part of the library's IT budget? Broken out by full-time equivalent student enrollment of the college.

Enrollment	No Answer	Separate line item in the library budget	Part of the library IT budget	Part of the college IT budget
Less than 2,500	18.75%	0.00%	50.00%	31.25%
2,500 to 7,499	6.67%	0.00%	53.33%	40.00%
7,500 to 14,999	7.69%	7.69%	46.15%	38.46%
15,000 or more	0.00%	0.00%	76.92%	23.08%

Table 7.5: About how much is in your library's annual central budget for the college library website?

	Mean	Median	Minimum	Maximum
Entire sample	$10,670.31	$0.00	$0.00	$100,000.00

Table 7.6: About how much is in your library's annual central budget for the college library website? Broken out by type of college.

Type of College	Mean	Median	Minimum	Maximum
Community college	$3,270.00	$0.00	$0.00	$37,000.00
4-year/MA-granting college	$13,800.00	$0.00	$0.00	$60,000.00
PhD-granting college/Research university	$20,222.22	$0.00	$0.00	$100,000.00

Table 7.7: About how much is in your library's annual central budget for the college library website? Broken out by public or private status of the college.

Public or Private	Mean	Median	Minimum	Maximum
Public	$11,285.71	$0.00	$0.00	$100,000.00
Private	$6,362.50	$225.00	$0.00	$25,000.00

Table 7.8: About how much is in your library's annual central budget for the college library website? Broken out by full-time equivalent student enrollment of the college.

Enrollment	Mean	Median	Minimum	Maximum
Less than 2,500	$5,214.29	$500.00	$0.00	$25,000.00
2,500 to 7,499	$50.00	$0.00	$0.00	$400.00
7,500 to 14,999	$6,312.50	$0.00	$0.00	$50,000.00
15,000 or more	$31,750.00	$18,500.00	$0.00	$100,000.00

Table 7.9: Total spending on the college library website in the past year has changed by approximately what percentage?

	Mean	Median	Minimum	Maximum
Entire sample	2.71%	0.00%	-20.00%	50.00%

Table 7.10: Total spending on the college library website in the past year has changed by approximately what percentage? Broken out by type of college.

Type of College	Mean	Median	Minimum	Maximum
Community college	-1.32%	0.00%	-20.00%	3.00%
4-year/MA-granting college	3.44%	0.00%	0.00%	17.50%
PhD-granting college/Research university	7.00%	0.00%	0.00%	50.00%

Table 7.11: Total spending on the college library website in the past year has changed by approximately what percentage? Broken out by public or private status of the college.

Public or Private	Mean	Median	Minimum	Maximum
Public	2.40%	0.00%	-20.00%	50.00%
Private	4.63%	0.50%	0.00%	17.50%

Table 7.12: Total spending on the college library website in the past year has changed by approximately what percentage? Broken out by full-time equivalent student enrollment of the college.

Enrollment	Mean	Median	Minimum	Maximum
Less than 2,500	-3.30%	0.00%	-20.00%	2.50%
2,500 to 7,499	2.50%	0.00%	0.00%	17.50%
7,500 to 14,999	0.00%	0.00%	0.00%	0.00%
15,000 or more	7.50%	1.00%	0.00%	50.00%

Table 7.13: Over the next year, you would expect that spending on the college library website will change by approximately what percentage?*

	Mean	Median	Minimum	Maximum
Entire sample	1.00%	0.00%	-20.00%	25.00%

Table 7.14: Over the next year, you would expect that spending on the college library website will change by approximately what percentage? Broken out by type of college.

Type of College	Mean	Median	Minimum	Maximum
Community college	-2.64%	0.00%	-20.00%	3.00%
4-year/MA-granting college	1.88%	0.00%	0.00%	10.00%
PhD-granting college/Research university	5.89%	1.00%	0.00%	25.00%

Table 7.15: Over the next year, you would expect that spending on the college library website will change by approximately what percentage? Broken out by public or private status of the college.

Public or Private	Mean	Median	Minimum	Maximum
Public	0.77%	0.00%	-20.00%	25.00%
Private	2.21%	0.05%	0.00%	10.00%

Table 7.16: Over the next year, you would expect that spending on the college library website will change by approximately what percentage? Broken out by full-time equivalent student enrollment of the college.

Enrollment	Mean	Median	Minimum	Maximum
Less than 2,500	-5.57%	0.00%	-20.00%	1.00%
2,500 to 7,499	1.12%	0.00%	0.00%	10.00%
7,500 to 14,999	0.83%	0.00%	0.00%	5.00%
15,000 or more	6.11%	2.00%	0.00%	25.00%

* Includes spending on salaries, technology, consultants, content development, etc.

Table 7.17: Over the past three years, how much did the library spend for outside programmers, consultants, and freelancers to alter, upgrade, or service in any way your academic library website(s) or your library social media sites?

Table 7.17A: Library website

	Mean	Median	Minimum	Maximum
Entire sample	$2,611.90	$0.00	$0.00	$50,000.00

Table 7.17B: Library social media sites

	Mean	Median	Minimum	Maximum
Entire sample	$0.00	$0.00	$0.00	$0.00

Table 7.18: Over the past three years, how much did the library spend for outside programmers, consultants, and freelancers to alter, upgrade, or service in any way your academic library website(s) or your library social media sites? Broken out by type of college.

Table 7.18A: Library website

Type of College	Mean	Median	Minimum	Maximum
Community college	$380.00	$0.00	$0.00	$4,000.00
4-year/MA-granting college	$3,076.92	$0.00	$0.00	$40,000.00
PhD-granting college/Research university	$4,571.43	$0.00	$0.00	$50,000.00

Table 7.19: Over the past three years, how much did the library spend for outside programmers, consultants, and freelancers to alter, upgrade, or service in any way your academic library website(s) or your library social media sites? Broken out by public or private status of the college.

Table 7.19A: Library website

Public or Private	Mean	Median	Minimum	Maximum
Public	$1,877.14	$0.00	$0.00	$50,000.00
Private	$6,285.71	$0.00	$0.00	$40,000.00

Table 7.20: Over the past three years, how much did the library spend for outside programmers, consultants, and freelancers to alter, upgrade, or service in any way your academic library website(s) or your library social media sites? Broken out by full-time equivalent student enrollment of the college.

Table 7.20A: Library website

Enrollment	Mean	Median	Minimum	Maximum
Less than 2,500	$444.44	$0.00	$0.00	$4,000.00
2,500 to 7,499	$4,000.00	$0.00	$0.00	$40,000.00
7,500 to 14,999	$0.00	$0.00	$0.00	$0.00
15,000 or more	$5,609.09	$0.00	$0.00	$50,000.00

Chapter 8: Web Statistics

Table 8.1: How many files are on your library's web site?

	Mean	Median	Minimum	Maximum
Entire sample	1,219.42	500.00	10.00	10,000.00

Table 8.2: How many files are on your library's web site? Broken out by type of college.

Type of College	Mean	Median	Minimum	Maximum
Community college	908.33	476.00	10.00	5,714.00
4-year/MA-granting college	1,296.18	500.00	130.00	3,700.00
PhD-granting college/Research university	1,508.30	325.00	25.00	10,000.00

Table 8.3: How many files are on your library's web site? Broken out by public or private status of the college.

Public or Private	Mean	Median	Minimum	Maximum
Public	1,108.32	500.00	10.00	5,714.00
Private	1,566.63	291.50	100.00	10,000.00

Table 8.4: How many files are on your library's web site? Broken out by full-time equivalent student enrollment of the college.

Enrollment	Mean	Median	Minimum	Maximum
Less than 2,500	187.50	115.00	12.00	452.00
2,500 to 7,499	2,090.33	500.00	120.00	10,000.00
7,500 to 14,999	1,009.70	500.00	10.00	3,700.00
15,000 or more	1,275.75	1,315.50	25.00	3,200.00

Table 8.5: How many unique visitors to the library website does your library site average weekly from September to May while college is in session?

	Mean	Median	Minimum	Maximum
Entire sample	50,108.64	8,000.00	500.00	950,887.00

Table 8.6: How many unique visitors to the library website does your library site average weekly from September to May while college is in session? Broken out by type of college.

Type of College	Mean	Median	Minimum	Maximum
Community college	141,661.89	3,000.00	500.00	950,887.00
4-year/MA-granting college	12,015.92	7,500.00	760.00	50,000.00
PhD-granting college/Research university	19,536.42	10,000.00	1,200.00	118,177.00

Table 8.7: How many unique visitors to the library website does your library site average weekly from September to May while college is in session? Broken out by public or private status of the college.

Public or Private	Mean	Median	Minimum	Maximum
Public	64,763.64	8,531.00	500.00	950,887.00
Private	4,311.75	2,800.00	734.00	10,000.00

Table 8.8: How many unique visitors to the library website does your library site average weekly from September to May while college is in session? Broken out by full-time equivalent student enrollment of the college.

Enrollment	Mean	Median	Minimum	Maximum
Less than 2,500	1,326.67	780.00	500.00	4,000.00
2,500 to 7,499	7,601.78	7,500.00	734.00	22,882.00
7,500 to 14,999	147,982.57	8,531.00	2,100.00	950,887.00
15,000 or more	49,211.91	17,000.00	2,867.00	288,387.00